Other Books by Joe Garner

We Interrupt This Broadcast
And the Crowd Goes Wild
And the Fans Roared
Echoes of Notre Dame Football
Stay Tuned

Now Showing

Unforgettable Moments from the Movies

Joe Garner

**Andrews McMeel
Publishing**

Kansas City

Now Showing copyright © 2003 by Garner Creative Concepts, Inc. All rights reserved. Printed in the United States of America. No part of this book may be used or reproduced in any manner whatsoever without written permission except in the case of reprints in the context of reviews. For information, write Andrews McMeel Publishing, an Andrews McMeel Universal company, 4520 Main Street, Kansas City, Missouri 64111.

03 04 05 06 07 QGR 10 9 8 7 6 5 4 3 2 1

Library of Congress Cataloging-in-Publication Data
Garner, Joe.
    Now showing : unforgettable moments from the movies /
Joe Garner.
        p. cm.
    ISBN 0-7407-3836-4
        1. Motion pictures—United States. I. Title.

PN1993.5.U6G33 2003
791.43'75—dc21

2003052150

Book design and composition by Holly Camerlinck

ATTENTION: SCHOOLS AND BUSINESSES

Andrews McMeel books are available at quantity discounts with bulk purchase for educational, business, or sales promotional use. For information, please write to: Special Sales Department, Andrews McMeel Publishing, 4520 Main Street, Kansas City, Missouri 64111.

To those who make the movies . . .
and to those who enjoy them.

Coming Attractions

Acknowledgments

A book like this is nearly impossible to do without the contributions of many talented and dedicated people. I am extremely grateful to Kathleen Andrews, John McMeel, Tom Thornton, and Hugh Andrews for their fervent commitment to our venture, and to Chris Schillig for her unwavering encouragement, enthusiasm, and guidance throughout the process. I feel privileged to be associated with such wonderful people and such a great publishing company.

A special thank-you to Abigail Ray, a woman who skillfully wears many hats at GCC. No task is too great or too small. She keeps the ship righted with her professionalism and enthusiasm, making it a joy to come to work.

Thank you to my agent, Sloan Harris, for his friendship and wise counsel.

I would like to extend my sincerest gratitude to Dustin Hoffman for contributing his enormous talent and integrity. I am honored and humbled to have him as host of the DVD.

I would also like to thank Lee Gottsagan at Punch Productions, and Dustin's attorney, Jill Smith, for all they did in helping to bring Dustin to this project. I am also grateful to Dustin's assistant, Aimee Nance, for skillfully coordinating the scheduling of the endless details that are inherent in this kind of endeavor.

Once again, I am grateful to designers Tim Lynch and Holly Camerlinck, copy chief Michelle Daniel, and administrative assistant JuJu Johnson of Andrews McMeel Publishing for their valued contributions of their talents and enthusiasm for making this book the best it can be.

Thank you to Chris Monte and Jim Castle for their uncompromising commitment to the quality of their work, and to Kris Wilson for his expertise and warm easygoing demeanor that kept us on track in the studio.

A special thank-you to Stephan Michaels for his creativity, boundless energy, and meticulous attention to detail. This book is better for it.

Thank you, as always, to my friend Wendy Heller-Stein for her willingness to share her expertise, open doors, and provide encouragement along the way.

Thank you to Andy Velcoff for his friendship, counsel, and his readiness to "make it happen" when we've been told it can't happen.

I am particularly grateful to Larry McCallister and Bill Berrios at Paramount Pictures, Chris Holm at Lucasfilm, Marlene Eastman at Warner Bros., Jess Wittenberg at Castle Rock Entertainment, Florene Kibbler at Twentieth Century Fox, Margarita Harder at Columbia TriStar Motion Picture Group, Joshua Baur at MGM, Jeremy Laws at Universal Studios, Bryan Patrick at Miramax Films, Robin Zlatin at New Line, and Steve Sellers at StudioCanal for permitting me to include these landmark motion picture moments.

Thank you to the following people for their determination in providing us with the very best images: Jeff Briggs and Woosley Ackerman at Warner Bros., Gilbert Emralino at Columbia TriStar, Kristoph Yniquez at Twentieth Century Fox, Deidre Thieman at Universal Studios, James Levine at American Zoetrope, Michelle Jouan at

Lucasfilm, Jeni Rosenthal at AP Wide World, Jonathan Hyams at MichaelOchsArchives.com, and Jay Williams at Shooting Star.

My gratitude to Melodie Moore and publisher Charles Koones of *Variety* magazine for generously providing archival articles that appear on the DVD.

My heartfelt thanks to Janel Syverud for always making sure that "my glass is half full."

I am always grateful to Bill Kurtis and Bob Costas for being there in the beginning.

And finally, none of this is possible without the incomparable strength and devotion I receive from my wife, Colleen, my son, James (J. B.), and my daughter, Jillian—they're the fuel of my soul; and to my parents, Jim and Betty Garner, for their never-ending love and encouragement; and Jerry and Sandi Barnes for their love and support.

Introduction

Why do we love the movies? Maybe because movies open a porthole to other places, other times, other worlds. We can journey to Oz and to outer space, check into the Bates Motel, follow Indiana Jones on his quest for a lost ark, fall in love with Ingrid and Marilyn and Meg, be terrified by great whites, and battle a Balrog in Middle Earth. Movies give us the chance to leave our lives behind and see the world as it was or is or could be. We love the power of moving pictures to move us—to laughter, to tears, to action. At special moments, we are at once transported and transformed.

I have always loved movies. It's a cliché, I suppose, but as a child growing up in the rural Midwest in the 1960s, I thought the movie theater was a magical place. Even small-town theaters were large and ornate. The big, heavy curtain rising as the lights went down made being there feel like an event. The dimming lights signaled an exit from one world as the parting curtain revealed the entrance to another. And in those days, we went to see the stars, not the special effects.

Whether you grew up watching films in theaters or in your family room, the one thing about movies that remains unchanged are their ability to affect us in ways unexpected and profound, especially when the movie includes a moment that clings to us as if cast by a spell, its impact undiminished by the passage of time.

Moments can be made memorable by a perfectly delivered line of dialogue, like "Here's looking at you, kid," or "I'll have what she's having." They may be memorable because they brought us nearly out of our seats with fright or laughter. Whatever the reason, we form an emotional connection and enjoy reliving those moments again and again.

This book and the accompanying DVD are a collection of moments that have become iconic in the history of motion pictures and woven themselves into the fabric of American culture.

The hardest part of compiling this material, of course, was deciding what to include and what to leave out. How could I account for every fan's notion of an unforgettable moment? If I ever finished such a book, you wouldn't be able to lift it. So for practical purposes, twenty-five seemed like the right number. Many of the choices seem self-evident, but in a few cases, the studio made the decision for me. For example, Lucasfilm was very generous and cooperative in allowing me to include *Raiders of the Lost Ark*. However, I was not given permission for *Star Wars*. So if you don't see one of your favorite moments here, it may not be for lack of effort on my part.

Here is another factor: Everyone who appears in the scenes on this DVD had to give permission before I could include any of his or her performances. Rounding up all those approvals made for some unforgettable off-screen moments as well. I trust that my assistant Abigail, an actress in her own right, will not soon forget her afternoon with Marlon Brando (who generously gave permission to include his entire soliloquy from *On the Waterfront*), and I will always treasure the hilariously candid conversation I had with Tony Curtis about how he and Marilyn prepared for that steamy seduction scene in *Some Like It Hot*. His story is in the book.

In fact, we were not always successful in tracking down every actor who appears here. A few were simply impossible to find. If you happen to be one of these elusive thespians, please contact me so that we can credit you properly.

Anyway, after culling through volumes of lists, polls, and surveys—including, I'll admit, my own list of favorites— I settled on these moments. I wanted the collection to span many genres and a wide era of time. Although these may or may not be the greatest moments in movie history, they are irrefutably unforgettable moments that have stood the test of time, scenes that have seared themselves into our hearts and collective imaginations.

I am extremely honored that two-time Oscar winner and seven-time nominee Dustin Hoffman agreed to introduce these moments on the accompanying DVD. For millions of movie fans, Dustin Hoffman is an inextricable part of many of their most unforgettable motion picture memories, from *The Graduate* to *Kramer vs. Kramer, Tootsie* to *Rain Man.* He's the quintessential actor's actor and a fine fellow to boot. Who better to present this collection?

A unique aspect of this format, I think, is that once you have had the opportunity to read the stories behind the memorable moment, you can watch it again, this time with perhaps a greater understanding and appreciation for what it took to create it.

I hope the stories in the book and the scenes on the accompanying DVD bring back some wonderful memories for you. Get comfortable, grab some popcorn, and let's go to the movies.

THE WIZARD OF OZ

1939

In the echelon of unforgettable movies and movie moments, MGM's fantasy musical *The Wizard of Oz* is perhaps the most unforgettable of them all.

With its simple heartwarming story of good versus evil, whimsical characters, elaborate and colorful fairy-tale sets, and dazzling visual effects, this 1939 film, brilliantly adapted from writer L. Frank Baum's best selling children's novel, was produced as a cinema spectacle on the grandest scale. It took a budget of $2.7 million, nearly one thousand costumes, six hundred actors, sixty sets, ten scriptwriters, four directors, endless creative battles, and state-of-the-art special effects to get the sweet and vulnerable Dorothy Gale from Kansas to Oz and home again.

L. Frank Baum's book *The Wonderful Wizard of Oz* (named for the O–Z letters on the bottom drawer of Baum's file cabinet) was a best-seller in 1900; he subsequently wrote a series of thirteen *Oz* books, a play that ran on Broadway for nearly three hundred performances, and an operetta. *The Wizard of Oz* was also twice made into silent films—first in 1910, then in 1925 with Oliver Hardy as the Tin Man—and into a cartoon short in 1933.

Fantasies were generally failures at the box office, but after the surprising success of Disney's animated feature *Snow White and the Seven Dwarfs,* MGM made the tactical decision to purchase the film rights to *Oz* for $75,000 in 1938. Elements from each of the various incarnations of Baum's work were borrowed for the MGM musical. From the 1902 play, screenwriters lifted the idea of a snowfall dampening the sedative power of the poppy field. The 1925 silent film introduced the notion of *Oz* as a dream with corresponding farmhand counterparts, and the 1933 cartoon initiated the concept of the transition from black-and-white into Technicolor.

The casting of *The Wizard of Oz* took months, and MGM was determined to cast as many of the major roles as possible from its own pool of 120 contract actors. Ultimately, though, the studio would have to look beyond its own stable of players to fill the roles of the Wicked Witch of the West, the Cowardly Lion, the Tin Man, Dorothy's Aunt Em, and the dog Toto. Hollywood's biggest star, Shirley Temple, was considered first for the role of Dorothy, but 20th Century Fox refused to loan Temple to MGM, so the studio turned to one of its freshest faces, sixteen-year-old Judy Garland.

Garland, valued by the studio more for her voice than her visage, had already made six movies in her two and a half years at MGM. W. C. Fields wanted too much money to play the Wizard, so character actor Frank Morgan got that role (along with Professor Marvel, the Emerald City doorman, the Emerald City cabbie, and the guard to the Wizard's throne room). For the Wicked Witch of the West, producer Mervyn LeRoy initially envisioned a glamorous witch modeled on *Snow White*'s evil queen and cast the beautiful actress Gale Sondergaard. When LeRoy was persuaded to make the witch ugly, the vainglorious Sondergaard bowed out and was replaced by Margaret Hamilton.

Vaudeville and Broadway song-and-dance man Ray Bolger was originally cast as the Tin Man but persuaded the Scarecrow, Buddy Ebsen, to switch roles during rehearsal. It was wonderful for Bolger's skills but ruinous for Ebsen—the aluminum dust powdering in the makeup for the Tin Man's face caused an allergic reaction that sent Ebsen to the hospital. Two weeks after shooting began, Jack Haley, a contract player from 20th Century Fox on loan to MGM, replaced Ebsen as the Tin Man.

To populate Munchkinland, MGM secured the services of Leo Singer, renowned proprietor of Singer's Midgets, a touring troop of acrobatic, singing, dancing, and wrestling midgets. MGM had hoped Singer could recruit two hundred little people but after scouring the country, Singer arrived in mid-November with only 124 midgets ranging in height from two feet, three inches to four feet, eight inches.

During the brief halt in production while Ebsen was hospitalized, LeRoy reviewed the early footage shot by the film's first director, Richard Thorpe. LeRoy found it bland and unmagical and fired Thorpe. Director George Cukor came on for one week before being moved to MGM's *Gone with the Wind*. Although Cukor did no shooting, he did make the decision to remove Garland's blond wig and heavy makeup.

Victor Fleming, an old-fashioned tough guy, directed the vast majority of the movie before he was sent to replace Cukor on *Wind*. One vintage Fleming moment came when Garland kept giggling at Burt Lahr's antics as the Cowardly Lion, ruining take after take. Fleming slapped Garland's face and sent her to the dressing room. Chastened, she soon returned and nailed the scene

in one try. After Fleming, King Vidor directed the black-and-white Kansas scenes.

The screenplay began with writer Herman J. Mankiewicz, who later wrote *Citizen Kane*. He decided to flesh out the book's Kansas scenes. Then Ogden Nash was assigned to the job but wrote nothing. Noel Langley and subsequently Florence Ryerson and Edgar Allan Woolf each took a turn at the screenplay.

Langley changed Dorothy's shoes from silver to ruby to maximize the Technicolor effect. But he originally scripted Auntie Em as the witchy one who wanted to be rid of Toto. And he focused the story too much on the Wicked Witch's battle for power against the Wizard. Gradually, Auntie Em was made more likable and Ryerson and Woolf—following the *Snow White* formula—shifted the drama to the Dorothy-versus-the-Witch dynamic.

The songs for *The Wizard of Oz* were integral to moving the story along. Songwriter Harold Arlen and his partner E. Y. "Yip" Harburg composed nearly forty minutes of songs, including "Over the Rainbow," "We're Off to See the Wizard," "Ding Dong, the Witch Is Dead," and "If I Only Had a Brain."

"If I Only Had a Brain" came quickly since Harburg simply wrote new lyrics for an unused melody from a previous show. But for Dorothy's yearning, aching song, "Over the Rainbow," Arlen struggled for a week before the right melody finally came to him while in a car outside Hollywood's famous Schwab's drugstore. Harburg found the tune for "Rainbow" too grand and mature for Dorothy, so they added the simple middle part with childlike notions of lemon drops and wishes upon a star.

During previews, studio executives looking to shorten the movie suggested cutting "Rainbow," deeming it unessential and beneath an MGM star to be singing in a barnyard. Associate producer Arthur Freed finally prevailed

upon studio boss Louis B. Mayer to restore the magical moment. Instead, "The Jitter Bug," a dance sequence that had taken five weeks and $80,000 to film, was clipped. Also cut was a long but wonderful dance sequence of Bolger's during "If I Only Had a Brain."

Filming was arduous under the blazing lights necessary for the brilliance of Technicolor. Garland's breasts were tightly bound and corseted to make her look younger, while Lahr, Bolger, and Haley spent two hours a day in makeup. The Cowardly Lion's outfit featured real lion pelt and weighed sixty pounds; Lahr sweated so much he needed two wigs made—while one got drenched with Lahr's perspiration the other was under a dryer. In his costume, Lahr couldn't open his mouth wide enough to eat and could only sip shakes and soup through a straw, or else endure another makeup application after lunch.

Bolger, who had a sponge-rubber mask attached by spirit gum to his face, couldn't remove his costume for lunch because the straw lumps had to remain in the exact same places. Haley's Tin Man outfit was so bulky he couldn't sit, only lean. Going to the bathroom was a major chore for all three men. And while Margaret Hamilton had it relatively easy, the green makeup tinted her skin for weeks after filming finished.

It took five weeks to make the costumes for all 124 Munchkins, while the famous ruby slippers were born from trial and error; spraying leather shoes red and painting patent leather were among a half dozen failed efforts before the costume makers attached red sequins to fine chiffon, then applied the chiffon on satin shoes.

Creating *Oz* required tremendous ingenuity and patience. Technicolor was so primitive that colors often appeared different on camera; the art department spent a week finding a yellow brick road that wouldn't look green, and every set, costume, and makeup design had to be tested.

Many of the visual effects that made for such memorable scenes as the twister tossing the farmhouse into Munchkinland; the transition from black-and-white to color; the six horses turning from white to green, blue, orange, red, then violet; and the disappearance and then melting of the Wicked Witch were surprising in their simplicity.

The farmhouse blowing away was accomplished by dropping a three-foot-tall miniature of the house from the soundstage ceiling, filming it in slow motion, and then reversing the image.

The transition from black-and-white to color was actually shot in color. Just before stepping into Munchkinland, Dorothy, with her back to the camera, is seen opening the brown farmhouse door, then stepping completely out of frame allowing for the revelation of the contrasting color splendor. The "Dorothy" with her back to the camera is actually Garland's stand-in, Bobbie Koshay, dressed in a black-and-white checked dress. Once Koshay was out of frame, Garland, dressed in the blue-and-white checked dress, stepped back into frame and through the door onto the color set.

After threatening to get Dorothy "and your little dog, too," the Wicked Witch vanishes in a burst of smoke and fire. Hamilton was pulled below the stage by a hidden elevator just before the flames shot up. The

shot worked fine the first time but after lunch Fleming wanted to try again and again. On the fifth take the flames burst too soon, the Witch's hat and broom caught fire, and Hamilton was out of work for six weeks with serious burns on her face and right hand.

Melting the Wicked Witch went a bit more smoothly. Again, Hamilton stood atop a hydraulic elevator, this time with dry ice inside her cloak. As she was lowered the ice's vapors made it look like she was melting, leaving just the costume behind. However, the first time, the elevator's compressed air blew Hamilton's hat off and her dress and cape over her head, so her dress had to be nailed to the floor.

Finally, to change the color of the horses in Emerald City, Jell-O powder was brushed into their coats.

The Wizard of Oz was a success but not an instant classic. Many mainstream magazines like *Time* and *Newsweek* gave good reviews but not raves, while intellectual critics called it heavy-handed and overwrought. The

New Yorker labeled it a "stinkeroo." Also, *Oz* was just one of 365 films released in 1939, including *Mr. Smith Goes to Washington, The Hunchback of Notre Dame, Stagecoach,* and, of course, *Gone with the Wind,* which dominated the media coverage and the Oscars, winning ten statues. (*Oz* won only Best Original Score.)

And while *The Wizard of Oz* was a commercial hit, grossing $3 million, the tremendous cast, new technologies, and promotional campaign drove final costs to nearly $4 million. The movie won new fans with a rerelease in 1948 but still, when Frank Morgan died the following year, most obituaries didn't even mention his *Oz* role. It wasn't until a deal with CBS in 1956 that initiated annual broadcasts of *Oz* that it became both profitable and an American icon. Generation after generation of children continue to revel in the wonderful magic of *Oz*, a movie that embodies the best of Hollywood—with a brain, a heart, and some nerve.

Unforgettable

MUSICAL MOMENTS

The Wizard of Oz was unforgettable because it was filled with wonderfully imaginative characters, lavish sets, elaborately staged production numbers, and hummable tunes. Here are other movie moments that have taken their rightful place in the annals of beloved Hollywood musicals.

Classic

Animal Crackers (1930) Not to slight the great Busby Berkeley extravaganzas but few musical spectacles have stood the test of time as well as Groucho Marx's singing of "I Must Be Going" followed by his dancing in "Hooray for Captain Spalding."

Swing Time (1936) Dance teacher Ginger Rogers urges "clumsy" student Fred Astaire to "Pick Yourself Up"—the perfect Depression-era message—then they strut their stuff in a scene with no frills but plenty of elegance, charm, and fancy footwork.

Holiday Inn (1942) Irving Berlin needed a song for each season; for winter he penned a little ditty called "White Christmas." Bing Crosby turned it into a timeless classic.

Yankee Doodle Dandy (1942) It's a collection of musicals within a musical, but James Cagney pulls off even the stagiest scenes like "Yankee Doodle Boy" and "Give My Regards to Broadway" with charm and élan. Not bad for an old gangster.

Singin' in the Rain (1952) Watch Gene Kelly leap onto the lamppost and you can't help smiling; watch him splash through the puddles and you'll want to rush out and join him.

Contemporary

Rocky Horror Picture Show (1975) "It's just a jump to the left . . ." and this instant cult classic was on its way to a "Time Warp" of never-ending midnight shows.

All That Jazz (1979) Styled after the inimitable Bob Fosse, Joe Gideon (Roy Scheider) dies with panache in "Bye-Bye Life," the exuberantly dark hallucination of a finale that ends with him zipped up in a body bag.

Little Shop of Horrors (1986) Originally a B movie with Jack Nicholson, this became an off-Broadway musical smash and then a movie musical. But it was never funnier than during Steve Martin's Elvis-style performance as the sadistic tooth puller in "Dentist."

This Is Spinal Tap (1984) When the dancing dwarf towers over the "Stonehenge" prop, the band finally realizes the disastrous shape they're in.

Moulin Rouge! (2001) The first Moulin Rouge scene feels like a vivid, feverish dream with its lush colors, adroit camera work, period dress, and anachronistic musical mélange—especially Nicole Kidman's Marilyn-to-Madonna medley.

From Stage to Screen

West Side Story (1961) Is it the opening dance sequence or "America" or "I Feel Pretty"? When a film wins ten Oscars, it's hard to pick just one great musical moment.

Music Man (1962) Robert Preston's brand of "Trouble" translated perfectly from his Broadway debut.

Sound of Music (1965) The hills truly are alive with Julie Andrews in this beloved movie's soaring opening scene.

Grease (1978) In the dark days of 1970s cinema, "Summer Lovin'" was a joyful paean to long-lost innocence.

MUSICAL MOMENTS CONTINUED

Rockers on Screen

Jailhouse Rock (1957) Elvis really was king when he wowed 'em with the rockin' title song, which he even choreographed.

Hard Day's Night (1964) For sheer musical exuberance, nothing matches the cinematic romp through the fields of "Can't Buy Me Love."

Tommy (1975) The story line is absurd, but director Ken Russell serves up a hypnotic, surreal visual feast to accompany Eric Clapton on "Eyesight to the Blind" and Roger Daltrey on "Listening to You."

The Blues Brothers (1980) Sure they were actors, but John Belushi and Dan Aykroyd were also genuine bluesmen as they proved with "Everybody Needs Somebody to Love" and their own "Jailhouse Rock." The movie also features songs by James Brown, Cab Calloway, Ray Charles, and a show-stopping Aretha Franklin with "Think."

Pink Floyd The Wall (1982) Pink Floyd's musical masterpiece incorporates indelible scenes like faceless children heading toward the meat grinder in "Another Brick in the Wall" and the animation of "Goodbye Blue Sky," in which a dove gradually morphs into a fighter plane.

Documentary

Monterey Pop (1968) Mama Cass sits in the front row astonished as Janis Joplin blows away the crowd with "Ball and Chain." Then the Who smash their equipment and Jimi Hendrix sets his guitar on fire. All in one movie!

Let It Be (1970) The Beatles' live rooftop performance—their final public appearance—is infused with a bittersweet poignancy that still rocks.

Woodstock (1970) Amidst some rough and ragged performances, the tight harmonies of Crosby Stills & Nash's "Suite: Judy Blue Eyes" brings some peace and love to Woodstock. And then there are the close-ups of Jimi Hendrix's hands playing "The Star-Spangled Banner."

The Last Waltz (1978) Despite a guest list that included Muddy Waters, Bob Dylan, and Eric Clapton, the Band proved this was their night with "The Night They Drove Old Dixie Down."

Stop Making Sense (1984) While their originals are hard to beat, the Talking Heads spirited reimagining of the classic "Take Me to the River" is truly joyous. Plus David Byrne wears his gigantic suit.

CASABLANCA

1942

It's an Academy Award–winning romantic melodrama set in the murky world of wartime espionage and regarded as one of the greatest movies in the history of American cinema. But when the camera began rolling, the script was unfinished, the supporting cast incomplete, the leading man disdained his character, and the leading lady pined for a different movie.

This is the unlikely recipe that produced the classic motion picture *Casablanca,* a perfect mix of romance, intrigue, and politics. The movie became a cultural touchstone and in the process transformed Humphrey Bogart, formerly pigeonholed as a tough guy, into a romantic idol and eventually an icon.

Bogart plays Rick Blaine, a cynical, supposedly apo- litical American café owner living in exotic Casablanca, content to sullenly drink and parry with the corrupt police chief, Captain Louis Renault. A thief named Guillermo Ugarte inadvertently bequeaths Rick valuable papers to help refugees escape the Nazis. Suddenly, Rick's long-lost love, Ilsa, shows up with her husband, Victor Laszlo, an anti-Nazi activist needing to escape. Rick is forced to shed his shell and confront the chaotic world around him. Bogart infused Rick with much of his own existential antihero persona, creating a symbol of America's rugged individualism and willingness to take a stand.

Casablanca is ranked among the greatest motion pictures ever made. That's quite a legacy for a movie born from a play that couldn't get produced. In 1938, New York City high school teacher Murray Burnett traveled to Vienna, where he witnessed the chaos and fear caused by Adolf Hitler's shadow, and then on to southern France, where he saw people partying in ignorance or denial.

Inspired by a visit to a cosmopolitan nightclub called La Belle Aurore that featured a black American musician, Burnett wrote a play called *Everybody Comes to Rick's*. (La Belle Aurore became the Paris café Rick and Ilsa visit.) The club also reminded Burnett of the 1931 show *Everybody's Welcome* and he incorporated a song from it, "As Time Goes By," into his script. (Composer Max Steiner, who wrote *Casablanca*'s score, loathed the song and fought unsuccessfully to replace it.)

Unable to find a theatrical producer for his play, Burnett took it to Hollywood. On December 8, 1941,

the day after Pearl Harbor was bombed, a Warner Brothers staffer read the play and recommended it highly to top producer Hal Wallis, even suggesting Bogart, James Cagney, or George Raft as ideal for the role. Wallis paid $20,000 for the rights, at the time the most ever for an unproduced play.

Ronald Reagan was the first actor publicly linked to the role when the Warner Brothers P.R. department sent out a news release announcing the film. But Wallis really wanted a world-weary, enigmatic tough guy—never Reagan's qualities—and had Bogart in mind from the beginning. In fact, when George Raft later lobbied Jack Warner for the role, Wallis said the part was specifically being tailored for Bogart. The veteran actor had starred in *High Sierra* and *Maltese Falcon* but had been largely stereotyped, stuck in crime and war movies as a tough guy—sometimes good, but usually bad.

Bogart was paid a handsome $36,000 for the role (the other stars earned $22,000 to $25,000), but early on he wanted out, disliking the dialogue, the scenes, and even Rick, calling him a cold and self-pitying whiner.

For Rick's love interest, Wallis tried and failed to get Ann Sheridan or Hedy Lamarr, so he turned to Ingrid Bergman, who took the part only because she'd failed to get the role she truly desired in the more literary *For Whom the Bell Tolls*. (But she subsequently landed that part, too.) Bergman was also unhappy with the script. By questioning Wallis and director Michael Curtiz, she helped push them to flesh out her character to resolve what she perceived to be gaps and contradictions.

Since the elegant Swede was no Lois Meredith, the part was renamed Ilsa Lund, and changed from a sophisticate to an innocent, a woman who believed her husband had died in a concentration camp.

Although Bogart and Bergman's magical chemistry was essential to the film's success, the two kept their distance off the set. Bergman had watched *Maltese Falcon* repeatedly before filming "so that when I met him I wouldn't be so frightened." But Bogart stayed aloof, largely because his wife, the alcoholic and jealous Mayo Methot, had threatened violence if she suspected an affair.

While the superlative supporting cast added depth

and humor to *Casablanca,* casting wasn't completed until well after filming started. One last-minute signing was Dooley Wilson as Sam, Rick's piano player and closest friend. Wallis almost changed the part to a woman, considering Lena Horne or Ella Fitzgerald, but decided that that relationship would be too risqué for 1940s audiences.

The cast featured people of thirty-four nationalities, many of whom had fled from Hitler's Europe: Paul Henreid had left Vienna; Peter Lorre (Ugarte), who was Jewish, left Germany; Conrad Veidt (Nazi Major Strasser), had a Jewish wife and had once been held under house arrest by the Nazis; S. Z. Sakall (Carl the waiter) was from Budapest; Madeleine LeBeau (Yvonne) was a refugee from occupied France; Marcel Dalio (Emil the croupier) also escaped France but learned during filming his parents had died in a con-

centration camp; and technical director Robert Aisner had escaped a German concentration camp and had journeyed through Casablanca en route to Hollywood.

When filming began on May 25, 1942, the script was only half finished. While Wallis admittedly threw the script together on the run, he did it shrewdly, hiring the studio's top writers and using their strengths. Writing independently, Philip and Julius Epstein, Casey Robinson, and Howard Koch tried to keep ahead of the shooting.

The Epsteins' contributions include Rick's retort when Strasser snidely asks if Rick can imagine the Nazis in Paris, London, and ultimately New York: "Well, there are certain sections of New York, Major, that I wouldn't advise you to try and invade."

Koch, wanting to infuse viewers with Rick's willingness to sacrifice, toughened up the character, chang-

"make her come to you. . . . You've got something she wants so she has to come to you." But it was necessary for the five-foot-four Bogart to slip on platforms when he wanted to stand level to look into Bergman's limpid eyes.

The constantly fluctuating dialogue and evolving characters frustrated the actors and created tension on the set. Bergman was particularly perplexed about not knowing how the film would end, always asking which man she'd end up with. No one told her, but Wallis and the writers knew she'd be leaving with Laszlo. Jack Warner wanted his two stars together, but killing Laszlo so she could stay with Rick seemed too pat, too Hollywood, and the censors of that era would never allow Ilsa to leave her husband for another man. The story that two endings were written is likely a myth.

ing him to an anti-Fascist activist, a man who'd supported underdogs but had lost his will after losing Ilsa. Watching Bogart play an ongoing game of chess by mail with an opponent in Brooklyn, Koch decided to make Rick a chess player—a strategic, thinking man.

Meanwhile, Robinson was brought in five days before shooting started to fix the love scenes. He replaced Ilsa's line "Hitler or no Hitler, kiss me" with "Kiss me as though, as though it were the last time," and he eliminated an exchange where Ilsa asks, "What is there about champagne?" and Rick responds, "The difference between bubbles or flatness—between life or death. The difference between having you or having nothing." He developed the scene where Ilsa threatens Rick before breaking down and admitting her love, leaving Rick to force her to live up to her own idealism.

Some of *Casablanca*'s most memorable moments came, however, from Bogart himself. The master script used the phrases "Here's good luck to you" and "Of all the cafés in all the cities in all the world . . ." Bogart is generally credited with changing those to lines more natural and in keeping with his character: "Here's looking at you, kid" and "Of all the gin joints in all the towns in all the world . . ."

Bogart was also open to suggestions. Unsure of how to play a romantic lead with such a beautiful woman, he followed a friend's advice to stand still and

But no one knew how to write the ending with style and in character. Near the end of shooting, it was decided to shift the final scene from the café to the airport. But the motivations remained murky and the writing appalling. Originally, the script called for Laszlo to beg Ilsa to come with him and for Rick to persuade Ilsa to leave by belittling himself. "I'm not the Rick you knew in Paris. . . . I serve drinks. I run a crooked gambling table. Every morning I lock myself in a room and drink myself dizzy. . . . I'm all finished. You belong to a fighter, not a saloon keeper."

But the script for the critical final scene gradually began to take shape. First Rick shed his self-loathing, saying, "You've given me back myself. And we'll always have that to remember. A few moments that were ours. . . . Inside of us we both know you belong to Victor. Maybe you'll hate me for it now, but you'll be thankful for the rest of your life."

But the lines lacked flair and the political motivation that took this beyond a mere love triangle. Finally, the night before shooting, the last touches were added, including unforgettable lines like "We'll always have Paris" and "You're part of his work," which make Rick noble and explains that romance doesn't always take precedence (or amount to a "hill of beans"). Filming the final scene wasn't easy, however: Bogart and Curtiz fought for hours over the delivery and went through dozens of takes—ultimately Wallis made them reshoot it another day.

The on-the-fly approach to writing the script also made it difficult to resolve some of the script's lingering problems. Why, for instance, were German couriers carrying letters of transit signed by General De Gaulle, leader of France's anti-Nazi forces? Why didn't the underground movement smuggle Laszlo out if he was so important? Why would a man of the underground and on the run show up at a popular nightclub with a white suit and a beautiful woman on his arm? And when the writers couldn't concoct a good reason why Rick couldn't return to America ("unpaid parking tickets," Julius Epstein jokingly suggested), they simply left it vague.

These unanswered questions prompted one critic to dub *Casablanca* "the best bad movie ever made" and another to dismiss its ultimate success as "the happiest of happy accidents."

But those remarks underestimate Wallis's and Curtiz's skills at navigating the studio's crank-them-out-quickly system. Curtiz, a Hungarian Jew who had fled anti-Semitism, was no auteur but he was prolific and proficient, directing some 165 movies, from *Yankee Doodle Dandy* to *Captain Blood* to *Mildred Pierce*. He paid attention to details large and small. Koch wanted the Paris scenes to flesh out Rick's anti-Nazi past, but Curtiz insisted on focusing on the lovers' relationship. And when Wallis wanted Bogart to go hatless in the outdoor scenes, Curtiz refused to change his mind, giving Bogart his signature look.

Wallis's imprint is felt from start to finish—he devised the newsreel opening to enhance the sense of importance, and—responding to audience previews—he ordered a new scene for the beginning to explain the letters of transit. Equally important, he didn't let a bad line linger. Wallis was unhappy with the film's last—and certainly one of its most memorable—lines, which was filmed as "Louis, I might have known you'd mix your patriotism with a little larceny." Two weeks after shooting it, Wallis called Bogart in to dub a new line he'd written himself, "Louis, I think this is the beginning of a beautiful friendship."

The movie was scheduled for a 1943 release but when the Allies landed in Casablanca on November 8, 1942, Warner rushed it out in New York with a huge publicity campaign. Enhancing its allure in January was President Franklin Roosevelt's trip to the Casablanca Conference. The movie earned rave reviews and audiences waited in line for hours all winter.

Bogart's forty-fifth movie role won him his first Best Actor nomination and *Casablanca* garnered eight Oscar nominations overall, winning for Best Picture, Director, and Screenplay.

Through it all *Casablanca* retains its powers to move, entertain, and inspire. After all, a classic is still a classic no matter how much time goes by.

HUMPHREY BOGART MOMENTS

Maltese Falcon (1941) After years of toiling in thug roles, Bogart became a leading man in *Maltese Falcon*. The movie's memorable last line was Bogart's idea. Borrowing from Prospero's speech in Act IV of Shakespeare's *The Tempest*, Spade dourly explains that the false Falcon is "the, uh, stuff that dreams are made of." But his first "Bogie" moment comes early on when Brigid O'Shaughnessy (Mary Astor) tries snowing Bogart's Sam Spade with her seductive charm: "You won't need much of anybody's help; you're good." Spade replies with a sneer, "It's chiefly the eyes and that throb you get in your voice when you say things like 'Be generous, Mr. Spade.'"

This scene encapsulates Bogart—his savvy, his open contempt for anything phony, and the flare in his eyes—and establishes the traits that made him an icon. Playing Spade, the one honest man in a world of thieves, led to *Casablanca*.

To Have or Have Not (1944) Bogart's most explosive scene comes when his character Harry Morgan, a cynical fishing boat captain, violently turns the tables on the arrogant French police. "You're both gonna take a beating till one of you uses that phone," he growls. "That means one of you is going to take a beating for nothing."

In Bogart's great noir movies, every line crackles with the threat of danger or sexual tension. His finest moment comes after his nineteen-year-old costar Lauren Bacall's sultry "Slim" delivers one of Hollywood's greatest lines; "You know how to whistle, don't you? You just put your lips together—and blow." She departs and Bogart's face shows bemusement then amusement as he ponders her offer then whistles once. The scene begat the storied Bogie and Bacall romance and solidified Bogart's image as a sexy leading man. Bacall had all the best lines, but this moment shows Bogart holding his own. Without words, he says it all.

This powerful speech foreshadows both McCloud's reluctance to act and the stand he ultimately takes for his principles. The politically active Bogart also neatly captures the mood of post-war America, while playing a showy monologue with characteristic restraint.

Key Largo (1948) When Johnny Rocco (Edward G. Robinson) first appears, Bogart's Frank McCloud rails against Rocco and the society that lets him flourish. He snarls that Rocco is "an emperor . . . whom he couldn't corrupt he terrified, whom he couldn't terrify he murdered," but the ex-soldier's bitterness is unmistakable when he quotes FDR's post–Pearl Harbor State of the Union, "We are fighting to cleanse the world of ancient evils, ancient ills."

This powerful speech foreshadows both McCloud's reluctance to act snd the stand he ultimately takes for his principles. The politically active Bogart also capyures the mood of post-war America, while playing a showy monologue with characteristic restraint

African Queen (1951) "What an absurd idea," Charlie Alnutt (Bogart) says, mimicking boat mate Rose Sayer (Katharine Hepburn). Then, sloppily drunk, Alnutt lets loose his pent-up fears and frustrations, climaxing by calling Rosie a "crazy, psalm-singing, skinny old maid" before singing himself to sleep.

Bogart had trouble getting into this loose role, director John Huston said, but he finally fully inhabited what Huston called "this wretched, sleazy, absurd, brave little man." Along with the scene of Bogie lying contentedly in Hepburn's arms cooing about love and his goofy impressions of hippos and monkeys, this moment demonstrated Bogart's range and earned him his only Best Actor Oscar.

Caine Mutiny (1954) On the witness stand at a court-martial trial he instigated, Bogart's Captain Queeg slowly unravels. As he denies mistakes, rants against disloyal officers, and slowly loses focus, the captain's face takes on a haunted quality that draws out the viewer's empathy without leaving Queeg's paranoia in doubt.

Bogart plays the decidedly unheroic captain's disintegration with even more depth and subtlety than he did Dobbs's breakdown in *The Treasure of Sierra Madre*. This scene revealed a Bogart willing to keep pushing himself and challenging audiences.

ON THE WATERFRONT

1954

"Who's going to care about a bunch of sweaty longshoremen?"
—DARYL F. ZANUCK

In the late 1940s and early 1950s, it was rare that 20th Century Fox studio head Daryl F. Zanuck made a major error in judgment. But with those casual words, he dismissed a fledgling project that would evolve into one of the most provocative, influential films in American cinematic history. Zanuck was wrong. People did care, and Columbia's *On the Waterfront,* the story of a morally conflicted dockworker who testifies against corrupt union officials, went on to enjoy immense popular and critical success, garnering eight Academy Awards and grossing more than $9.5 million in its initial release.

Based on reporter Malcolm Johnson's series of Pulitzer Prize–winning articles about unionization on the New York waterfront, Budd Schulberg's script was a stark meditation on the evils of unchecked authority and the redeeming power of love. It also produced what is arguably Hollywood's greatest dramatic scene between two men. The legendary "I coulda been a contender" taxicab confrontation between Marlon Brando and Rod Steiger was a beautifully condensed scene on the film's themes of loyalty and betrayal; the tension-fueled dialogue revealed two artists at the height of their powers and cemented Brando's reputation as the most innovative actor of his generation. "If there is a better per-

formance by a man in the history of film in America," wrote director Elia Kazan of Brando in his autobiography, "I don't know what it is."

Brooding and brutish, oscillating between tough-guy bravado and disarming tenderness, Brando's shiftless exboxer Terry Malloy shuffles through life as an errand boy for murderous union boss Johnny Friendly, played by Lee. J. Cobb, and his right-hand man, Terry's older brother Charley, played by Steiger. But when Terry falls for Edie Doyle, portrayed by Eva Marie Saint, whose brother was murdered by Friendly's goons to prevent him from speaking out about union corruption, Terry is forced to examine whether his cushy job is worth the bloodstained paycheck.

Encouraged by Edie and crusading waterfront priest Father Barry, played by Karl Malden, Terry eventually turns on his paymasters, testifying before the crime commission and leaving his brother to the mercy of the union boss's gun thugs.

Despite the brilliance of its performances—every major actor in the movie was nominated for an Oscar—and the technical virtuosity of its production, *On the Waterfront* was much more than a celluloid masterpiece. Upon its release in July 1954, the film attracted as much attention for its real-life subtext as it did for its grim, convincing portrayal of proletarian strife on the docks.

Two years earlier, during the ongoing investigation by the House Un-American Activities Committee (HUAC) into communist influence in the film industry, Kazan had been called to testify. When asked by the committee to provide names of alleged communists and communist sympathizers, he did. Schulberg had done the same the previous year. The hearings polarized the Hollywood community and led to the blacklisting and deportation of a number of prominent artists. Kazan and Schulberg earned the ire of many who felt they should have kept their mouths shut. Neither man apologized.

The personal implications were hard to ignore. *On the Waterfront* was widely seen as the pair's polemical defense of their HUAC testimonies. "Snitch," "stool pigeon," "canary," "rat"—all the epithets heaped on Terry Malloy for his actions were also leveled at Kazan and Schulberg. And while Schulberg has denied there

was a specific intent to address the HUAC issue in the film, Kazan had a different take on the situation. Recalling his feelings on Oscar night in 1954, the director later wrote, "I was tasting vengeance that night and enjoying it. *On the Waterfront* is my own story; every day I worked on that film, I was telling the world where I stood and my critics to go and [——] themselves."

Among those critics was Marlon Brando. Having worked with Kazan on *A Streetcar Named Desire* (1951) and *Viva Zapata!* (1952), the actor felt a personal obligation to the director, but he turned down the role of Terry on principle. Brando reconsidered after Frank Sinatra was tapped for the part. "Politics has nothing to do with this," producer Sam Spiegel reportedly told him to assuage his guilty conscience. "It's about your talent; it's about your career." Brando took the role on the condition that he could leave the set most days at 4 P.M. to visit his psychoanalyst.

The grueling thirty-six-day shoot began on the frigid Hoboken docks in November 1953, an arrangement that pleased Kazan because he felt the extreme cold gave the actors a realistic, "miserable" look. Undoubtedly, both cast and crew were relieved on the day of the taxi scene because the shoot took place inside a studio. But if the weather had been momentarily conquered, other problems were just beginning.

To start, the notoriously stingy Spiegel refused to spring for an actual cab on the street, deciding that filming in traffic would consume too much time and money. Instead he delivered to Kazan the busted-out shell of half a cab. Adding insult to injury, the producer also failed to arrange for back projection, which would have created the illusion of a busy street outside the cab's rear window. Kazan was left with a bleak studio wall.

After some quick thinking, the crew hung a venetian blind—an unusually upscale touch for a New York taxi, but one that serendipitously added to the intimacy of the scene. To create the illusion of movement, crew members rocked the cab shell back and forth while others, at the urging of cinematographer Boris Kaufman, waved various objects in front of the lighting to simulate oncoming headlights.

The scene hit another snag when the cameras started rolling. From the beginning, Brando strayed from the script, improvising in a way that left Steiger (who has said he was a "nervous wreck") confused and bewildered. Several times, Kazan interrupted the actors and had them start again, before calling a halt to the filming to speak with Brando about his bold display of artistic license.

After a brief consultation between the actor, director, and Schulberg, in which Brando proposed script changes (particularly in the way he should react to the gun in the scene), the actors tried again. This time, Kazan got what he was looking for.

What the cameras captured was nothing less than the pure distillation of the entire morality tale; it is unquestionably the heart of the film. Steiger and Brando play it perfectly as brothers who, despite their deep love for one another, find themselves on opposite ends of a deadly moral struggle from which neither is willing or able to escape. The tenderness and sorrow with which Brando disarms the gun-toting Steiger, leaving him no option but to feebly surrender and face his doom, lend a heartbreaking quality to the scene that is crystallized in Brando's anguished lines: "I coulda had class, I coulda been a contender, I coulda been somebody."

According to Steiger, the sibling rivalry wasn't confined to the script. After filming a wide shot with both actors in the frame and then Brando's close-ups over Steiger's shoulder, Kazan let Brando leave for psychoanalysis, telling Steiger the actor was tired and needed to rest. Humiliated and on the verge of tears, Steiger was forced to perform his close-ups for the scene with the film's dialogue supervisor, Guy Thomajan, standing in for Brando. Years later, Steiger said it was the worst thing one actor could do to another.

Kazan has admitted that he offered very little in the way of direction once the scene got going, letting the actors play it as they saw fit. Steiger, perhaps still smarting from Brando's slight, described the experience years later as "two people in combat." For his part, Brando told writer Truman Capote in 1957 that they had to

shoot the scene six or seven times because Steiger, overcome with emotion, could not stop crying.

Characteristically, though, Brando was hardest on himself. Indeed, he was so displeased with his own performance that after a screening for Leonard Bernstein, who later composed the score, he walked out without a word. He subsequently confided to Karl Malden that he thought his acting was rough and uneven.

The Academy and the public saw it differently. *On the Waterfront* collected eight Oscars, including a Best Actor nod for Brando, as well as Best Picture, Best Director, Best Story and Screenplay, Best Supporting Actress for Saint, Best Black-and-White Cinematography, Best Black-and-White Art Direction, and Best Editing.

Today the film stands as one of the best American motion pictures ever made.

MARLON BRANDO MOMENTS

Marlon Brando has been called an "actor's actor," an icon of American cinema. Here are his most influential screen roles:

A Streetcar Named Desire (1951) "Stell-laahhhh!" Marlon Brando didn't just turn in a star-making performance in *Streetcar;* his new school of naturalism, with its "method acting" approach, changed film acting forever. While Brando's work is electrifying throughout, this scene, with the primitive Stanley in a wet, torn T-shirt bellowing for his love, is the one seared into the minds of everyone who saw the film.

The Wild One (1953) This movie about bikers marauding through a small town and the townsfolk's simplistic overreaction may seem tame and even a bit dated, but it was a shocker in its day. The film was banned in England and became the source of much mainstream consternation in the United States. Every antiestablishment film that followed, from *Rebel Without a Cause* to *Easy Rider,* traces its roots to *The Wild One.* Indeed, much of the social upheaval of the 1950s and 1960s seems to reflect this movie's view, which is exemplified in the scene when a girl asks Brando's Johnny Strabler, the biker leader, "What are you rebelling against?" He cocks an eyebrow and shoots back, "What've you got?"

The Godfather (1972) By the early 1970s, Marlon Brando was no longer considered bankable in Hollywood. *The Godfather* not only became an American classic, it reaffirmed Brando's place in the acting firmament. The film begins with Brando as Don Vito Corleone at his daughter's wedding, revealing both his power and the Godfather's system of honor and respect in an unforgettable scene that lays the foundation for the movie and its sequels. With menace and sorrow in his voice he tells a supplicant, "You say, 'Don Corleone, give me justice.' But you don't ask with respect. You don't offer friendship. . . . Instead, you come into my house on the day my daughter is to be married, and you ask me to do murder for money." It is a chilling, eye-opening scene.

Last Tango in Paris (1972) This controversial film about Paul, a middle-age American widower, and Maria, a twenty-year-old French girl, who meet for anonymous, empty sex is remembered for its sex scenes and the use of butter for forced sodomy. Brando's most memorable scene is usually noted as his out-of-control monologue over his wife's dead body. In fact, his finest moment comes in a quiet scene when he reveals his past to Maria (Maria Schneider), mesmerizing viewers with the story of his unhappy childhood, which Brando is said to have based on his own youth. It's a simple scene that rings true and reminds viewers of Brando's ability to hold our attention no matter what he is saying.

Apocalypse Now (1979) He weighed nearly three hundred pounds, had his head shaved, and seemed deranged. Without Brando's eerily riveting performance as the crazy, murderous Colonel Walter Kurtz in this journey into the heart of darkness, the film would have failed. "I've seen the horrors, horrors that you've seen. But you have no right to call me a murderer. You have a right to kill me—you have a right to do that—but you have no right to judge me." When Brando delivers those lines, it is impossible not to believe him or understand the reason behind the mission to assassinate him.

SOME LIKE IT HOT

1959

Some Like It Hot, the movie classic ranked number one on the American Film Institute's list of 100 Greatest Comedies, had its origins in a low-budget stinker of a 1951 German film called *Fanfares of Love,* in which two guys desperate for jobs put on blackface to get into a band and, at one point, dress up as women. It was a movie that director, cowriter, and producer Billy Wilder called a "terrible picture . . . deliriously bad."

What was Wilder's brilliant twist on this "deliriously bad" German film? He used it to turn the real-life St. Valentine's Day Massacre—a brutal, gangland slaughter carried out by Al Capone's Chicago henchmen in 1929—into a comedy.

The idea wasn't an easy sell. As Billy Wilder told

Cameron Crowe in Crowe's book *Conversations with Wilder,* he went to fabled producer David O. Selznick with his idea, and Selznick was horrified. "Oh, my God," he said. "You're not doing a comedy with a murder in it. They're going to crucify you." But the German director, who had a penchant for very dark comedy, forged ahead, enlisting renowned screenwriter I. A. L. "Iz" Diamond to help him craft the script.

That they were able to fashion a successful screenplay around such disparate elements was proof of their genius. They knew instinctively that in order to get away with the massacre, they first needed a way to hook the audience—give them someone to root for. That element came in the characters of Joe and Jerry, played by Tony Curtis and Jack Lemmon, the hapless unemployed musicians who were unwitting witnesses to the crime.

Wilder explained to Crowe, "We did some comedy at the top, then . . . the massacre, and they [the audience] swallowed it because they were with me already. The two guys, Lemmon and Curtis, up on the stage playing those instruments . . . that set the mood that allowed us to spill a little blood." It didn't hurt that the hood orchestrating the hit was played by famed movie gangster George Raft (who, as a side note, is killed in the movie by none other than Edward G. Robinson Jr., son of the prototypical film gangster).

Of course, the casting of the dashing and versatile Tony Curtis, the multitalented Jack Lemmon, and movie goddess Marilyn Monroe was central to the project's success. Somewhat surprisingly, the original choice for the role of Sugar Kane Kowalczyk was not Monroe. It was Mitzi Gaynor, the '50s musical comedy star whose most famous role remains Ensign Nellie Forbush in the film version of *South Pacific*. But when Wilder got word that Monroe, who'd starred for him in *The Seven Year Itch*, wanted the part, he moved mountains to get her.

Though Frank Sinatra had originally been considered for the role of Jerry/Daphne, it was Jack Lemmon who won that part. This was Lemmon's first movie with Wilder, and the director admired his work so much that Lemmon became one of Wilder's favorite leading men, starring in his classic films *The Apartment*, *Irma la Douce*, and *The Fortune Cookie*.

Film veteran Joe E. Brown, who'd made dozens of low-budget films and was retired and nearly forgotten, was cast as the loopy millionaire, Osgood Fielding III. By chance, Wilder spotted Brown at a Dodgers game and knew immediately that he had found the perfect actor to play Fielding, Jerry/Daphne's "love interest."

Like its two gender-bending lead characters, *Some Like It Hot* is a film in which all is not what it seems, and that extended to the film's location. The hotel and beach scenes, supposedly set in Florida, were actually shot at the Hotel Del Coronado, an architectural gem built in the 1880s on the Pacific Ocean near San Diego, California.

Since the beach was public, there were always hundreds of fans on the sand watching the filming. For her part, Marilyn Monroe loved the adulation, and the crowd supplied it nonstop. The fans were constantly screaming and whistling for her attention. Monroe had such power over them that when Wilder needed quiet for a take, he would have her go "Shhhh," and the throng would obediently go silent.

If Monroe had power over her fans, she had less

power over her own demons. Her personal life was a shambles. She was in the last stages of her marriage to playwright Arthur Miller, and she was battling psychiatric and substance-abuse problems. She'd often show up hours late or not at all, but she was so valuable to the movie that Wilder and the entire cast and crew had to make it work somehow. They often didn't know which Marilyn Monroe would show up—the consummate pro or the addled star. According to Curtis, the director warned him and Lemmon, "Don't let me catch you with your thumb in your rear end, 'cause if it happens to be during the take that Marilyn nails, that's the one I'm printing."

Sometimes Monroe's recitation of the simplest lines required as many as eighty takes. As Wilder recalled for Crowe, "You have to remember, when a man muffs a line, and they do it again and again and again, then you replace him. . . . Marilyn was the star. She does the take because it's gonna be in the picture."

On the other hand, Monroe could be flat-out amazing, as in the scene on the beach when she first meets Tony Curtis with his Bronx-tweaked Cary Grant accent, pretending to be Junior, the heir to Shell Oil. The scene had three full pages of dialogue that translated into three minutes of screen time. Curtis and Monroe had to do it in one take because there were

seaplanes taking off nearby every three or four minutes. They nailed the scene the very first time. Wilder says that when the take was over, Monroe was so shocked that she'd gotten through the scene she almost fainted.

For all her idiosyncrasies, Monroe knew what was best for her professionally. She was radiant on camera, and she knew it. And she knew how to protect her image. When she first met the actresses playing the Sweet Sues, the all-girl band in the movie, she was introduced to one girl who had blond hair. Not just blond hair like a lot of other girls have—it was Monroe's shade of platinum blond. Monroe went to Wilder and said, "No other blonde. I'm the only blonde," and the girl had to dye her hair.

One key to Monroe's immortal performance, Wilder said, was that she had "a kind of elegant vulgarity about her. That, I think, was very important. And

she automatically knew where the joke was. She did not discuss it. She came for the first rehearsal, and she was absolutely perfect, when she remembered the line."

The costumes were also a vital component of *Some Like It Hot*, which was originally titled *Not Tonight, Josephine*. Monroe handpicked Australian designer Orry-Kelly to design her gowns. The diaphanous form-fitting numbers, especially the one she wore during the seduction scene with Curtis on the yacht, are considered some of the sexiest creations ever worn by an actress in a movie. In fact, after Tony Curtis and Jack Lemmon scoured the costume department and found nothing that really fit, they, too, called upon Orry-Kelly to clothe their "girlish" figures.

Though *Some Like It Hot* was nominated for five Oscars, including Best Director for Billy Wilder and Best Actor for Jack Lemmon, Orry-Kelly was the only winner. He took home the 1959 Academy Award for Best Costume Design, Black-and-White.

One of the scenes Billy Wilder is most proud of plays out aboard Osgood Fielding's yacht, where Curtis brings Monroe to seduce her. Wilder and cowriter Diamond thought the scene was too flat. Then Wilder woke up one night with a brainstorm—they would make Curtis pretend to be impotent! Monroe, mixing the motives of pity and greedy opportunity, seduces Curtis. What could be sexier than that?

Curtis and Monroe, who had been linked romantically years earlier, loved the idea for the scene. "I went to her trailer to rehearse. We agreed that it would be 'no holds barred,'" says Curtis. "She told me how much she loved Cary Grant and I told her how much I loved her." When the two stepped onto the set, "We were like two prizefighters ready to spar. It was pure, raw passion," says Curtis.

The most ingenious part of the scene, designed both to reveal Junior's reaction and to skirt the censors, involved his left leg. As Curtis feigns disinterest, his leg, which is behind Monroe's back, rises, telling

the whole story. While Curtis plays it cool, his telltale leg tells all.

Billy Wilder was famous for ending his films with an unexpected twist. Indeed, one of his most famous and most perfect closing lines comes at the end of *Some Like It Hot*. Amazingly, it's one that Diamond had tossed off the night before— something they threw in as a placeholder until they could find a "better line."

It was spoken by Joe E. Brown, as the wealthy, oft-married Osgood Fielding, to his affianced Daphne, Jack Lemmon in drag, as they motor out to his yacht. Behind the wheel, Brown smiles beatifically as Lemmon, increasingly more frustrated, gives him one reason after another that marriage is impossible for them. Brown blithely counters every impossibility he throws out. Finally, at his wit's end, Lemmon says, "You don't understand, Osgood," pulls off his wig, turns to Brown, and yells, "Aaaah . . . I'm a man."

Without missing a beat, Brown throws back the film's final line, "Well, nobody's perfect," leaving a perplexed Lemmon, and the audience, to ponder.

Brown was right; nobody's perfect. But in the history of film, *Some Like It Hot* may just be the perfect comedy.

BILLY WILDER MOMENTS

Billy Wilder was an immigrant who found the pulse of America. He veered from charming romance to sardonic drama without missing a beat. He had a way with words and with the camera. Wilder was, undeniably, one of the greatest writer-directors of all time.

Double Indemnity (1944) An insurance man and a femme fatale plot to sell her husband extra insurance then murder him. As this crackling film noir classic hurtles toward its climax, the perfect murder unravels and in a darkened living room the coconspirators turn on each other. "We're both rotten," Phyllis Dietrichson (Barbara Stanwyck) tells Walter Neff (Fred MacMurray). "Only you're a little more rotten," he retorts. Moments later she shoots him. Wounded, he dares her to finish him off. "Maybe if I came a little closer?" When she breaks down and instead embraces him, he shoots her point-blank, coldly saying, "Good-bye baby."

Sunset Boulevard (1950) The most quoted line comes near the end when the delusional Norma Desmond (Gloria Swanson) descends the staircase for what she believes is a return to stardom and says "I'm ready for my close-up," but the scene that exemplifies Wilder's brilliance as a storyteller is actually the opening. Wilder sets the tone for this tale of power, fame, and illusion with a startling first scene: As audiences see police rushing to a mansion and fishing the dead body of writer Joe Gillis (William Holden) out of a swimming pool, the narrator dryly informs them that a murder has been committed and we will flash back in time to learn the true story. Except, of course, the narrator is the dead man.

Stalag 17 (1953) Sergeant J. J. Sefton (William Holden) looks out for himself, and himself alone. So when it turns out there's a traitor in the barracks of this World War II POW camp, it isn't surprising that Sefton is a suspect—but Wilder scores points about mob mentality and Hitler's followers as everyone gangs up on Sefton. The crucial scene comes when Sefton gets his first clue as to the real villain's identity. Wilder deftly orchestrates the action. While the other men parade around singing "When Johnny Comes Marching Home," Sefton is isolated on his bunk. He sees the shadow of the lightbulb dangling and a lightbulb goes off in his own head. It is simultaneously funny and tense—Wilder at his best.

The Seven Year Itch (1955) Marilyn Monroe (her character doesn't even have a name) is chatting idly about a movie *(The Creature of the Black Lagoon)*, but who really cares what she's saying? All that matters is that she stands over a subway vent to cool her ankles and the breeze blows her dress up. The scene comes and goes quickly and there's less leg than in the movie poster that cemented the image in our collective imagination, but sex appeal doesn't get any better than this.

The Apartment (1960) Jack Lemmon plays Baxter, a schlub who gets ahead in the corporate world by letting higher-ups use his apartment for their affairs while he skulks around outside losing sleep and catching colds. When we see Baxter surrounded by other nameless office workers, his nose dripping, his face twitching, selling his soul by working the phones trying to please each immoral and manipulative boss, we know that even if he wins he'll lose.

PSYCHO
1960

"He wouldn't harm a fly . . ."
—NORMA "MOTHER" BATES

By 1960, Alfred Hitchcock had long since established himself as the master of suspense with such complex thrillers as *Rear Window*, *Vertigo,* and *North by Northwest*. The movie for which he's best remembered, however, is the low-budget, black-and-white horror film called *Psycho*. In the minds of those who have seen it, the mere mention of the title instantly conjures up images of the knife-wielding killer and the shrill sound of screaming violins. And in spite of Hitchcock's parsimonious approach to making *Psycho*, the film has left an indelible mark on the way movies are made and how they are marketed.

Inspired by the wave of popular B movie horror thrillers in the late 1950s, Hitchcock set out to make a no-frills film that met his own high standards. With minimal rehearsal time and at a cost of only $800,000, *Psycho* was shot in black-and-white instead of Technicolor by the crew of the Hitchcock television show *Alfred Hitchcock Presents,* who were accustomed to working cheap and fast.

The movie was adapted from Robert Bloch's 1959 novel *Psycho,* which was inspired by the monstrous murders of real-life Wisconsin serial killer Ed Gein. Bloch's Norman Bates was, like Gein, bald and middle-aged. Hitchcock and screenwriter Joseph Stefano set about adding their own distinctive touches to the psychotic

killer. Hitchcock's vision for Bates was actor Anthony Perkins, a budding young star with matinee-idol good looks. The change in physical traits transformed the character of Bates from sick and scary to vulnerable and empathetic. And although Hitchcock couldn't have known it, Perkins was the archetypal Norman—an only child whose father had died when he was five and whose mother was eccentric and overbearing.

Perkins reportedly added several vital touches to his character, including several pieces of telling dialogue like, "A boy's best friend is his mother. She—she had to raise me—all by herself, after my father died. I was only five and it—must've been quite a strain for her. . . . A son is a poor substitute for a lover."

Another crucial difference is that in the novel, Mary Crane—whose name was changed to Marion in the film when a real Mary Crane was discovered in the Phoenix phone book—drives straight from Phoenix to the Bates Motel with no diversions along the way. Hitchcock loved what he called "MacGuffins," his name for something the audience thinks is important but really isn't. The first half hour of the movie is the ultimate MacGuffin. When Marion, played by Janet Leigh, steals $40,000 for her lover Sam, played by John Gavin, so he can afford to marry her, Hitchcock makes the audience believe this conflict will be the heart of the movie. It isn't until Norman Bates murders Marion that viewers realize the film's true theme.

Audiences were also distracted by Hitchcock's risqué flourishes. While the director deglamorized Marion by having Leigh wear off-the-rack dresses costing only what a secretary could afford, he also made her extremely sexual. In 1960 women didn't appear on film without a slip. Hitchcock, having decided that younger filmgoers had a new set of mores and conventions, pushed the boundaries—first dressing Marion in white lingerie as a "good" woman with her lover, then in black lingerie after she steals the money.

While the lingerie was an eyeful, censors were more up in arms about the scene in which Marion throws a scrap of paper into the toilet. No one had ever shown a toilet on the big screen before, and Stefano and Hitchcock not only fought for its inclusion but also insisted on showing it being flushed.

The most demanding, controversial, and memorable scene of all was, of course, the shower scene. While Hitchcock shot the entire film in six weeks, a complete week was devoted to the forty-five-second shower scene, which required seventy different camera setups and a multitude of key considerations.

Blood was a central element in the scene and the right substance had to be used for filming in black-and-white. Hitchcock chose chocolate syrup because of its similar density to real blood.

The sound the knife made during the attack was equally crucial to Hitchcock. The director had someone stab different types of melons while he looked away. Ultimately, a casaba melon produced what he determined to be the suitable sound for the stabbing.

Costumers looked though striptease magazines for an outfit that would make Leigh appear naked, settling on a nude-colored moleskin. A professional nude model, Marli Renfro, was paid $400 to be Leigh's body double for the week, testing whether the camera would pick up the nudity through a shower curtain and the flow of water. Although Hitchcock

said Renfro's legs and stomach appear in several shots, Leigh has insisted that she appeared in every cut in the shower scene and that Renfro appeared on film only when Norman wrapped Marion's dead body and dragged it to the car.

Despite Hitchcock's careful editing, Hollywood censors insisted they saw nudity and knife-on-flesh contact in the stabbing scene and demanded that Hitchcock remove it. Hitchcock argued that he had

directed the scene to fool viewers into thinking that's
what they saw, but insisted that there was no actual
nudity. In the end, Hitchcock said he'd "make the
changes," but simply resubmitted the scene unaltered,
and the censors passed it through.

Most challenging of all was filming Marion's eye
after her death. Hitchcock ordered a special contact lens
for Leigh, making the eye appear unblinking and
glazed. When he learned it would take six weeks for
Leigh's eye to grow accustomed to the lens, he told the
actress she would just have to hold extremely still.
However, with no automatic focus, the camera had to
be adjusted by hand as it pulled back from the close-up
of her eye; getting it right took two dozen takes. On
the last take, when the camera worked properly, Leigh's
moleskin began to pull loose, exposing her naked body
underneath. According to Leigh, she was so determined
to complete the scene that she held her head still even
as the male crew was getting "more than an eyeful."

Hitchcock's frugality motivated his decision to
experiment with minimal scoring throughout *Psycho*,
allowing the ambient sounds of each scene's location to
underscore tension and emotion. Even for the iconic
shower scene Hitchcock ardently stated to his composer, Bernard Herrmann, that he wanted only the
sound of the shower combined with the stabbing and
Marion's screams to be heard. Herrmann grudgingly
followed Hitchcock's mandate in all scenes *except* the
shower scene. But the director was so pleased with
Herrmann's violent violin score that he rewarded the
composer by nearly doubling his salary.

Psycho's other big surprise, of course, was Mother,
Norma Bates. Hitchcock kept the set closed to out-
siders and spread rumors about casting for the role of
Norma Bates just to throw off snoops; Helen Hayes
was among those he supposedly considered for the
part. After filming, Hitchcock used trailers and promotional photos that falsely implied that Marion's sister
Lila, played by Vera Miles, gets killed and that Marion
encounters Mother.

Again, Hitchcock's attention to sound was critical
in creating tension and surprise. For Norma Bates's

voice, he didn't want audiences to recognize Perkins, so he used three actors—Paul Jasmin, Virginia Gregg, and Jeanette Nolan (married to John McIntire, who played Sheriff Al Chambers)—blending their voices together, sometimes switching back and forth from word to word. Norma was "played" by a midget when Perkins carried her downstairs and by other women for the murder scenes.

For the final touch, when Norman "finds" the body and shouts "Mother! Oh, God, Mother! Blood . . . blood," Hitchcock had the bass removed from Perkins's voice to make him sound strangely adolescent.

As the effects staff created different models for Norma's corpse, Hitchcock would sneak the bodies into Leigh's dressing room chair—partly to test which got the best reaction and partly to keep Leigh feeling as edgy as Marion.

Norma's big moment in the basement was quite difficult to film because a cameraman had to squat just out of sight behind her chair as it and the camera spun around, terrifying Lila and the audience.

Determined not to allow the details to leak out, Hitchcock extended his authority beyond the gates of the studio and into the theaters themselves. He revolutionized movie marketing by demanding that theater owners not allow audiences into their theaters once the movie had started. The thrill of *Psycho* depended on the MacGuffin setup, and he didn't want people who arrived after Marion was killed to complain that Leigh wasn't in the film. Hitchcock's bold stipulation caused grumbling, but the gambit worked.

All his manipulations and scares earned Hitchcock some harsh reviews; *Newsweek* dismissed *Psycho* as a "gimmick movie" and the *New York Times* called it a "blot on an honorable career." Despite the panning from the press, Hitchcock had a huge hit on his hands, and *Psycho* has schooled a generation of filmmakers in the craft of heart-pounding suspense.

Following *Psycho*, Hitchcock directed *The Birds* (1963), *Marni* (1964), *Torn Curtain* (1966), *Topaz* (1969), and *Frenzy* (1972). He ended his distinguished fifty-year career with *Family Plot* in 1976. Perkins went to Europe until 1965. Upon returning, he was frequently typecast and ultimately gave in, playing Norman Bates in three *Psycho* sequels. Leigh had several more hits, including *The Manchurian Candidate* (1962), but *Psycho* forever marked her, too. After seeing herself attacked in the shower scene, Leigh never again felt comfortable taking a shower.

For audiences and cast members alike, it seemed that once you checked into the Bates Motel, you never really checked out.

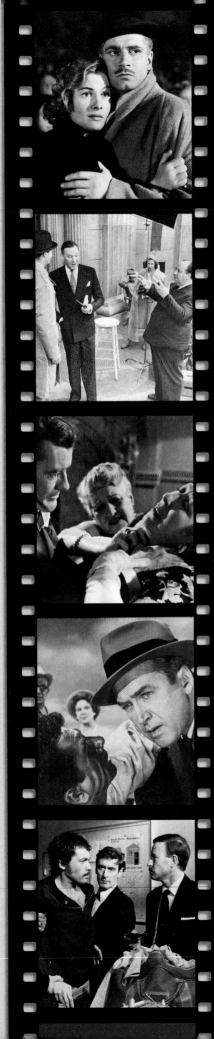

ALFRED HITCHCOCK MOMENTS

Director Alfred Hitchcock is responsible for many memorable movie scenes. The most famous of the master's moments—from *Vertigo*, *North by Northwest*, *Rear Window*, *Saboteur*, *The Birds*, and, of course, *Psycho*—are not just icons, they are essential elements in the language of cinema. However, Hitchcock was responsible for plenty of thrills and chills beyond those classics; here are five underrated Hitchcock moments.

Rebecca (1940) Hitchcock's first American movie was his richest, deepest, most emotional film and won him his only Best Picture Oscar. Joan Fontaine plays the second Mrs. de Winter, whose life is haunted by Maxim de Winter's (Laurence Olivier) late first wife, Rebecca. Rebecca drowned in a boating accident, but her beauty and charm still seem to permeate both Maxim's heart and every inch of his mansion, Manderley. When Rebecca's boat is suddenly recovered, Maxim confesses to his new wife that her body will be found. "I put it there," he says, confessing that he actually loathed Rebecca and is haunted by guilt, not love. This is a shocking revelation, but in true Hitchcock fashion, it is not the end—he still has another twist or three in store.

Foreign Correspondent (1940) In this story of a cop reporter turned foreign correspondent, John Jones (Joel McCrea) chases down an international plot to gain key diplomatic secrets on the eve of war. This film features one of Hitchcock's most brilliant twists ever. On an airplane escaping to America, villain Stephen Fisher (Herbert Marshall) and his do-gooder daughter Carol (Laraine Day) receive a wire that he is to be arrested and learn that Jones, who loves Carol, and pal Scott ffolliott (George Sanders) are on board the plane. This seems like the climax, but suddenly the plane is attacked from the sea and goes into a terrifying, spectacular crash. As the survivors clutch onto a too-crowded wing, Stephen Fisher shows some heroism, plunging into the stormy seas so the others can live. And to think that Hitchcock made this one the same year as *Rebecca*.

Strangers on a Train (1951) Only Hitchcock could intertwine an innocent sport like tennis with a mundane incident like a man reaching for a cigarette lighter that has fallen into a sewer and build unbearable tension into the scene. Bruno (Robert Walker) is a sociopath who proposed a murder swap to tennis star Guy (Farley Granger); Guy dismisses the idea but Bruno goes ahead with it anyway, murdering Guy's wife and demanding Guy kill Bruno's father. In the end, Bruno is desperate to frame Guy and is rushing to the scene of the crime to plant evidence—the lighter—when he drops it down the sewer. Meanwhile, Guy nervously tries to finish off a tough tournament foe so he can sneak off to prevent Bruno from planting the lighter. Then Hitchcock tops it all off with a final fight scene on an out-of-control merry-go-round.

The Man Who Knew Too Much (1956) In one of Hitchcock's true gems, Dr. Ben and Jo McKenna (Jimmy Stewart and Doris Day) inadvertently become embroiled in an international assassination plot, only to find that their son has been kidnapped by the killers. At Royal Albert Hall in London, they race to stop the murder, which viewers know will come at the crash of the cymbals. The rising tension as Stewart rushes down the hall is perfectly edited to match the music. Then the wordless scene is punctuated not by the bang of the cymbals or the shot from the gun but by Day's terrified scream.

Frenzy (1972) In Hitchcock's last top-notch film, he returned to London as the setting. The story revolves around a man falsely accused of being the "Necktie Strangler," but the best scenes involve the real criminal. Bob Rusk (Barry Foster) realizes that his latest victim, whom he has shoved into a burlap sack filled with potatoes and dumped on the back of a truck, died clutching Rusk's monogrammed stickpin. He crawls into the back of the truck and struggles to pull the corpse out, but the truck driver climbs behind the wheel and heads out onto his route. Tension escalates as the truck bounces and swerves, the potatoes spill, and Rusk frees the nude corpse only to find that rigor mortis has set in, and he must break the fingers to loosen their grasp and win his race against time.

THE GRADUATE

1967

The Graduate is a classic countercultural film with a twist—a romance where the hero gets the girl after sleeping with her mother. Set to the music of Simon & Garfunkel, the movie resonated with a generation coming of age during the chaotic '60s—alienated from the values of their parents but, like the movie's central character Benjamin Braddock, worried about their future.

The Graduate was released in 1968, and the timing was perfect. While the movie lightheartedly portrayed seduction and adultery, it still hit the raw nerve of the generation gap and became the ultimate pop movie about disaffected youth. In addition, the movie launched star Dustin Hoffman, director Mike Nichols, screenwriter Buck Henry, and musicians Paul Simon and Art Garfunkel into stardom.

The movie begins with Benjamin fresh out of college, confused and concerned about his future, wanting it to be "different"—a concern that openly spoke to the 1960s generation. Although Ben falls prey to the predatory seduction of Mrs. Robinson, the wife of his father's business partner, Ben's real rebellion is in disobeying Mrs. Robinson by pursuing her daughter Elaine, refusing to accept the elder's rigid decree that he's not good enough for her daughter.

The movie was adapted from a 1963 novel titled The Graduate by Charles Webb. After reading an article about Webb in the New York Times and recognizing the film potential of Webb's novel, movie producer Lawrence Turman quickly bought the rights.

Turman hired writer Buck Henry, creator of the hit TV spy spoof *Get Smart,* to write the screenplay. Ironically, Henry was never entirely satisfied with the movie's most famous line. When one of Benjamin's father's friends cryptically offers Benjamin unsolicited career advice, he tells him, "One word: plastics." Henry meant to convey the artificiality and superficiality of the older generation; "plastics" was a 1950s term for phony and it was no longer considered hip, but Henry was unable to find a better one-word substitute.

Then Turman hired director Mike Nichols, who at that point had never directed a movie and had directed only one Broadway play. Yet Turman believed Nichols's direction of *Barefoot in the Park* had exactly the smart and clever tone he wanted for *The Graduate*. However, because the project took so long to get off the ground, Nichols first directed *Who's Afraid of Virginia Woolf?* before starting Turman's project.

Turman and Nichols initially clashed over casting.

The book portrayed the Braddock family as beautiful Southern California blonds—"surfboards" as Buck Henry called them—and Nichols wanted young Robert Redford, who he'd worked with in *Barefoot*. At that point, the role of Mrs. Robinson was offered to Doris Day, and Candice Bergen was being considered for Elaine. But while Webb's vision of Benjamin was handsome, Turman wanted someone sweet, awkward, and insecure. He argued that Redford was too much the matinee idol. Turman and Nichols screen-tested Redford, and Nichols concurred.

Several other young actors were tested, including a stage actor from New York who was the very opposite of Webb's Braddock, Dustin Hoffman. Hoffman arrived at his screen test exhausted, nervous, and without his lines memorized. He felt even worse after he was forced to spend two hours in makeup with Nichols, who wanted Hoffman's eyebrows plucked, his nose shaded, and his neck thinned with a turtleneck.

Feeling demeaned, Hoffman was then thrust into a romantic scene with Katharine Ross, whose natural beauty made him even more nervous. The low point for Hoffman was when he accidentally touched Ross's rear end, and she quickly told him to keep his hands to himself. Hoffman thought the screen test was a disaster, but his insecurities and addled emotions conveyed exactly what Turman and Nichols wanted for Benjamin.

With Hoffman cast, everyone else was hired to fit the same look—less blond, more ethnic. Concerned for her image, Anne Bancroft, who at thirty-six was not even seven years older than Hoffman, was advised by everyone except her husband, Mel Brooks, to reject the part.

Nichols conceived of one other innovative bit of casting from the start. Pop or rock music rarely showed up in a movie unless it was about musicians, such as the Beatles' *A Hard Day's Night*. Nichols knew that he not

only wanted to flaunt that convention but he also wanted the popular duo of the day Simon & Garfunkel, whose lyrics captured the mind-set of the era. Turman commissioned three new songs from Paul Simon, but the singer-songwriter was too busy and managed to write only enough of "Mrs. Robinson" to complete the film. The other Simon & Garfunkel songs used in the film, like "Sound of Silence," had already been recorded.

Coming from a theatrical background, Nichols provided an extra three weeks of rehearsals before the cameras started rolling, demonstrating patience as the inexperienced Hoffman, who was accustomed to projecting from a stage, struggled to find his footing. Nichols encouraged Hoffman to act naturally and allow the camera to capture his emotions.

Nichols also found other successful avenues into

Hoffman's psyche. For the scene in which Benjamin asks for a room at the hotel, which featured screenwriter Buck Henry as the desk manager, Nichols heightened Hoffman's nervousness by telling him to imagine he was asking a female pharmacist for condoms.

In the first love scenes with Bancroft, Nichols asked about the first time Hoffman had ever touched a girl. The actor told of an old school trick of sticking his arm through his coat sleeve timed to "accidentally" grab the breast of a passing girl. Nichols had him channel that immaturity in shooting the pair's first encounter, and Hoffman walked over and put his hand on Bancroft's breast. Bancroft was shocked, and Nichols burst out laughing. Hoffman got a case of the giggles; to regain control, he walked to a wall and banged his head on it. Nichols thought the head banging was part of Benjamin's character and used it in the movie.

Nichols was equally adroit with the camera, creating an innovative visual look. When Mrs. Robinson lures Benjamin into her sun porch, we hear him utter his famous line, "Mrs. Robinson, you're trying to seduce me," through the arch of her bent leg. Like most of the film's unusual shots, this was not just a visual gimmick—Nichols used his camera technique to effectively convey what the characters were thinking or feeling.

When Bancroft put her foot up on the stool during a break, Nichols—who viewed Mrs. Robinson as a tiger stalking her prey—saw the sexy leg as the tiger's trap for Benjamin. As soon as he saw it, he shot it that way and didn't bother with any extra takes or angles. Mrs. Robinson was also dressed in stripes, and the room was filled with plants, like a jungle.

Nichols also influenced the story itself. In Webb's novel, Benjamin crashes Elaine's wedding before it ends, and they race off into an exciting future. Nichols found that too corny, so he had Benjamin arrive after the vows and steal Elaine away, completely flouting traditional societal values.

Many critics believed that the shot of Hoffman

The Graduate was the biggest hit of 1968, earning $50 million and seven Academy Award nominations, although only Nichols took home a statue. Paul Simon had resisted finishing "Mrs. Robinson" and releasing it as a single before the film's release, but he quickly recorded a full version of the song and rushed it out, earning three Grammy Awards for him and his partner, Art Garfunkel.

In the following years, the participants and other producers have bandied about possible ways to film a sequel to this classic; Buck Henry even parodied the idea in a scene in Robert Altman's *The Player*. Nothing has yet come of these ideas and *The Graduate* is left with its uncertain ending to symbolize an era of uncertainties. So for now, Ben and Elaine still face an ambivalent fate that's both timeless and frozen in time.

banging on the glass window with his arms spread apart was meant to be symbolic of Jesus on the cross, but the reality is much simpler. The glass seemed as if it was going to break when Hoffman banged on it with his fists closer together, and the clergyman said that if they didn't stop shooting it that way he would put an end to the filming. So Hoffman spread his arms and pounded the glass with his palms as a means of defusing the pressure.

Nichols then went even further in undermining Hollywood's typical happy ending. When Benjamin and Elaine first make their escape in the back of a city bus they look giddy and elated, but as they head off, reality settles in and their joy fades into a confused quiet. Nichols, who believed Benjamin and Elaine were not rebels and would end up just like their parents in ten years, captured the moment by telling the actors to sit on the bus without any further direction. Then he just let the camera roll and roll and roll and the actors, who had no scripted parts, wore the same look of bemused doubt that Nichols wanted from the characters.

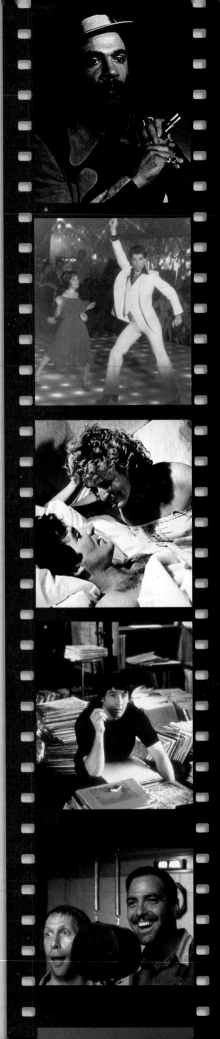

MOVIE SOUND TRACKS

The sound track to *The Graduate* was an integral part of the movie's success, and many of its Simon & Garfunkel compositions went on to become anthems of the era. The sound track album was certified gold on March 27, 1968. It was number one for nine weeks and remained on the charts for a total of 69 weeks. Here are other sound track albums that were as important to their films and as influential in their time.

Superfly (1972) In the aftermath of the inner-city riots of the 1960s came black power and a wave of so-called blaxploitation movies. Those trends have faded, but the music of the title track, "Superfly," the hit "Freddie's Dead," and "Pusherman" remain vibrant three decades later. The reason? Curtis Mayfield. Unlike most hodgepodge sound tracks, *Superfly* reflects the vision of one legendary artist at his creative peak. Mixing strings, horns, funkadelic guitar, and percussion with gritty, honest lyrics, this sound track effectively captures black America's frustration, fear, hope, and yearning.

Saturday Night Fever (1977) The gold standard. The sound track that inspired the sound track craze. *Saturday Night Fever* sounds as good today as it did in 1977, when it ignited the disco craze. Strip away the hype and you'll find an irresistible album featuring a surprising number of classics. The most memorable and worthy tracks are, of course, from the Bee Gees—"Stayin' Alive," "Night Fever," "Jive Talkin'"—but "If I Can't Have You" and even frothy romps like "Boogie Shoes" and, yes, "Disco Inferno," will have you singing and dancing along.

The Big Chill (1983) This sound track—a repackaging of old Motown and rock hits—may not have started America's lust for nostalgia, but it certainly capitalized on it. The movie and its songs perfectly captured the longing for a wild and carefree youth. Since songs like "I Heard It Through the Grapevine," "The Tracks of My Tears," "Natural Woman," and "A Whiter Shade of Pale" are all worthy of their status as classics, this sound track is a great listen even for someone who never lived through the 1960s or saw *The Big Chill*.

High Fidelity (2000) A movie about a record-store owner who loves making mix tapes should spark high expectations for its sound track, and *High Fidelity* comes through, with a mix of underrated songs by celebrated stars (Bob Dylan, Stevie Wonder, the Kinks), cult favorites (Velvet Underground), and newer indie bands (Smog, Stereolab). Even the cover art—an homage to the Beatles' *A Hard Day's Night*—is on target. The only thing missing is a sequel album, since the movie featured nearly sixty songs, and this gem has but fifteen.

O Brother, Where Art Thou? (2000) In a high-tech, fast-paced, glitz-is-good era, *O Brother* was a ray of sunshine. It breathed new life into country, bluegrass, folk, gospel, and other roots music, including such staples as "You Are My Sunshine" and "I'll Fly Away" and forgotten tunes like "I Am Weary" and "O Death." The simple, honest tunes made stars of musicians Alison Krauss, Gillian Welch, and Ralph Stanley and awakened the music industry, which generally ignores such traditional sounds.

FIVE EASY PIECES

1970

When *Five Easy Pieces* opened in 1970, the movie was hailed as a vivid reflection of its time, one that mirrored a widespread sense of restlessness and frustration at the close of the '60s. These days it's best remembered as the picture that turned Jack Nicholson into a star.

Five Easy Pieces ushered in an era of visionary, independent-minded directors telling complex, character-driven stories—a time when Francis Ford Coppola, Robert Altman, Roman Polanski, Terrence Malick, and John Cassavetes flourished. The movie has also been credited with inspiring male actors to show a raw vulnerability, since the film was largely dependent on Nicholson's willingness to bring humanity to a flawed, essentially unlikable character. "You've got to keep attacking the audience and their values," Nicholson once said. "If you pander to them, you lose your vitality."

At the end of the 1960s, Nicholson was little more than a B-movie veteran, starring in such instantly forgotten films as *The Wild Ride* and *The Terror*. In fact, it was only when the frustrated thespian turned to writing in 1968 that his fortunes changed. Nicholson cowrote the script for *Head,* a psychedelic film starring the Monkees, with director Bob Rafelson. When Nicholson acted out his ideas, Rafelson was so impressed that he decided to find Nicholson a worthwhile role.

Still, even Rafelson didn't know what he had. As producer of *Easy Rider,* he cast Rip Torn as lawyer

George Hanson, sending Nicholson to the set merely in an informal advisory role. But when Torn dropped out, Nicholson stepped in, winning raves for his scene-stealing performance. Now Rafelson understood Nicholson's unique talent and began working with writer Carole Eastman, who had known Nicholson for years, to tailor a script specifically for his skills and personality. (Eastman used the pen name Adrien Joyce.)

Nicholson is a skilled, often subtle actor, and much of his best work—the rebel in movies like *One Flew Over the Cuckoo's Nest* and the conflicted sufferers of *The Crossing Guard* and *About Schmidt*—is foreshadowed in *Five Easy Pieces*. The movie tells the story of Bobby Dupea, a former piano prodigy who walked away from his destiny feeling overwhelmed by the expectations of his father, himself a musical genius. But now Bobby doesn't know how to stop running.

When the movie opens he is working as an oil-field rigger with a lifestyle and girlfriend he doesn't respect and is ready to drop at a moment's notice. Suddenly, however, his life becomes more complicated than he can handle. His girlfriend, Rayette (Karen Black), becomes pregnant, and his father is incapacitated by a stroke, compelling Bobby to pay a visit to the suffocating, isolated family compound where his older brother and sister still live and pursue their father's musical dreams.

The film moved beyond *Easy Rider* in demonstrating that hippies weren't the only people who were disillusioned with and felt disconnected from American society; the quest for personal fulfillment was universal

and often smacked right up against the coldness of the real world.

Bobby's character brims with energy and candor, but also cruelty, selfishness, and irresponsibility. Eastman based Bobby on her brother and on Nicholson himself—indeed Bobby's temper and skills at Ping-Pong and bowling all parallel the veteran actor's. Nicholson had also confounded expectations, turning down a college scholarship for Hollywood where he toiled for many years.

Even the movie's most famous scene was inspired by Nicholson, who had a real-life argument with a waitress at a Hollywood hangout, Pupi's, that ended when he trashed a pastry cart. The film creates more than a simple diner dispute, however. Bobby's seething rebellion is incited by a hitchhiker who has been rant-ing about American society while riding north with Bobby and Rayette. When the waitress (Lorna Thayer) remains rigid in refusing to serve Bobby his off-the-menu order of toast, Bobby loses his cool.

He politely asks for a chicken salad sandwich on toast, no mayonnaise, no butter, no lettuce, and hold the chicken. "You want me to hold the chicken?" the waitress repeats. "I want you to hold it between your knees," Bobby retorts. Then in one sweep, he clears the table, sending water glasses and menus flying.

But Bobby isn't just a mindless rebel. The scene culminates in the car when the hitchhiker lavishes him with praise only to be stopped by Bobby's quiet admis-sion that he made his point but lost the battle. "I didn't get [my order], did I?"

The film's other emotional centerpiece didn't come

as naturally to Nicholson. Toward the end, Bobby wheels his muted father to an open field where he opens his heart to him, apologizes for failing to meet the family's standards, and confesses that he understands his restless dissatisfaction but can't resolve it.

"My life—most of it doesn't add up to much that I could relate as a way of life that you could approve of. I move around a lot, not because I'm looking for anything really, but to get away from things that go bad if I stay. Auspicious beginnings, you know what I mean. . . . The best that I can do is apologize. . . . I'm sorry it didn't work out."

This scene precipitated a serious conflict between

Nicholson and Rafelson. Rafelson wisely wanted to make Bobby empathetic or at least less unlikable before the film's disturbing finale, so he told Nicholson to cry during the scene. Nicholson, who had already marked up the scene in his script, preferred a tuned-down approach, dismissing tears as self-pity; he also rebelled against being told to act a specific emotion.

Rafelson argued that Bobby was "crying because of his agony over the life he was leading and that this agony had to be revealed." Nicholson finally agreed, but added personal touches in rewriting the script—the terse "auspicious beginnings" was a reminder of his own years of hardship as an actor. And when it came time to cry, Nicholson churned up his feelings for the man he believed was his own father, an alcoholic, who played almost no role in raising him. When he died, Nicholson did not attend his funeral. (Nicholson later learned this man was really his grandfather, that his "mother" was his grandmother, and that his "sister" was his real mother.) Later, Nicholson called this raw emotion a "breakthrough," both for himself and for other leading men.

Art and real life intersected again on *Five Easy Pieces* in Nicholson's affair with Susan Anspach. The actress had been offered the part of pregnant Rayette but found it too cutesy and instead chose to play Catherine, the independent-minded piano student engaged to Bobby's buffoonish brother. Bobby has a fling with Catherine, simultaneously reaching for emotional salvation and undermining it by flaunting his own sense of failure. During the filming, Nicholson and Anspach had a brief, intense affair, almost as stormy as their on-screen pairing. They went their separate ways as soon as filming ended, but remained forever connected. Anspach skipped the film's New York premiere in September 1970

because she was about to give birth. Nicholson later acknowledged the boy, Caleb, as his son.

Rafelson overrode Eastman with the movie's conclusion. She wrote an ending alluding to Ted Kennedy's Chappaquiddick accident: Bobby dies but Rayette survives when their car crashes off a bridge. But the scene struck a false note with the director and star. Nicholson wanted Bobby to walk away on his own, but Rafelson went one better. In a gas station bathroom, Bobby looks in a mirror and can't face up to himself. He abandons his car, his belongings, and his girlfriend to hitch a ride with a trucker heading to Alaska.

Despite the downbeat ending, the movie won a huge following, earning Oscar nominations for Nicholson and Black as well as for Best Original Screenplay and Best Picture. Shirley MacLaine said that the diner scene made Nicholson her acting hero, and *Newsweek* put the new star on its cover, calling him a Marlon Brando and James Dean for the 1970s. Of course, looking back across the decades, it's easy to see that Nicholson became much more than that. He became Jack.

JACK NICHOLSON MOMENTS

No other actor has had more Oscar nominations or a more colorful screen persona than Nicholson. These may not be his best movies, but they all capture the essence of Jack.

Chinatown (1974) Jake Gittes puts his life—and his nose—on the line to unravel corruption in Los Angeles. Finally closing in on the crime, he tells his client Evelyn Cross Mulwray (Faye Dunaway), "There's no time to be shocked by the truth." When he slaps the truth out of her, he learns that the mystery girl, Katherine (Belinda Palmer), is really both her sister and her daughter. Nicholson's acting is especially stunning here because, in real life, he had just learned that his family was not who he thought they were.

One Flew Over the Cuckoo's Nest (1975) The rigid Nurse Ratched (Louise Fletcher) won't alter hospital routines to let rebellious Randle McMurphy watch the World Series. When McMurphy wins the votes of his fellow patients, Ratched keeps finding technicalities to justify her unbending adherence to the rules. Undeterred, McMurphy stands in front of the blank TV and begins announcing an imaginary game. His spirit is contagious, and the others start "watching" and cheering the "action." For one glorious moment, they are all set free.

The Shining (1980) Nicholson's character is writer Jack Torrance, who spends the winter with his family as caretaker of the sprawling Overlook Hotel. Snowed-in, all that work and no play makes Jack gradually go insane. The most indelible moments come when he axes his way toward the bathroom where his wife, Wendy (Shelley Duvall), is hiding, maniacally bellowing, "Then I'll huff and I'll puff . . ." and "Wendy, honey, I'm home," and finally, "Heeeeere's Johnny."

A Few Good Men (1992) As Colonel Nathan Jessep, Nicholson channels his ferocity and intensity into the ultimate establishment figure. But he hasn't sold out. On the stand in a memorable showdown with Navy lawyer Lt. Daniel Alistair Kaffee (Tom Cruise), he reveals the dangers of giving institutional power to such a man. Defending his dubious decisions and bawling threats like, "I'm gonna rip the eyes out of your head and puke in your dead skull," Nicholson makes it clear that Jessep is the one with blinders on, the one who "can't handle the truth."

The Crossing Guard (1995) This may be a flawed film, but Nicholson's performance as Freddy Gale, who responds with grievous, vengeful rage to his daughter's killing by a hit-and-run drunk driver, is masterful. Nicholson's ex-wife, Mary, is played by Anjelica Huston, whose real long-term relationship with Nicholson had just ended badly. The frostiness in their scenes together is palpable; the first one starts with disquieting tension, then quickly escalates. Later, as Gale is breaking down, he reaches out to Mary, but when she says she pities him, he turns on her saying, "I hope you die." It isn't pretty, but it feels as raw and real as anything Nicholson has ever done.

DIRTY HARRY

1971

DISTRICT ATTORNEY: *"It's the law."*
DIRTY HARRY: *"Well, then, the law is crazy."*

In the late 1960s, a serial killer known as "The Zodiac" cut a swath of terror through the San Francisco Bay Area, executing randomly selected victims, sending cryptic messages detailing his brutal crimes to local newspapers, and taunting the police for their inability to track him. He was never caught.

Moviemakers have often been tempted to solve on-screen those problems that seem most intractable in real life. At a time when America witnessed an unprecedented rise in violent crime and political corruption, director Don Siegel's *Dirty Harry,* inspired by the Bay Area's murderous psychopath, gave the public just what it clamored for: a hard-nosed cop with an itchy trigger finger who was as disgusted with spineless bureaucrats as he was with criminals—a cop who would take care of business and let the chips fall where they may.

The script, which was written by Harry Julian Fink and Rita M. Fink and later reworked by Dean Riesner, follows San Francisco Police Inspector Harry Callahan as he hunts down the Zodiac-inspired Scorpio killer (played by a convincingly deranged Andy Robinson), who has threatened to prolong his kidnapping and murder spree unless the city pays him $200,000. Chagrined by the mayor's decision to "play this creep's game" and put up the ransom, Callahan resolves to put the clamp on Scorpio using his own rather unconventional tactics.

Callahan's vigilante style did not sit well with some,

and *Dirty Harry* drew immediate fire from a number of prominent critics not only for its ultraviolent plot and gratuitous nudity, but also for its apparent disdain for constitutional rights and its perceived reactionary, racist—even fascist—underpinnings. Such condemnations did little to deter audiences, however, who thrilled to Eastwood's portrayal of Callahan on the rampage—perpetually pissed off but always cool, busting down doors, torturing perpetrators, bad-mouthing his superiors, and distractedly munching hot dogs as he picked off violent criminals with his cannon-like handgun.

Of course, rogue lawmen and vigilantes were nothing new in American film; since the 1930s, Westerns and police films had brimmed with iconic pistol-packing loners intent on bringing bad guys to justice, even if it meant trampling on the law a bit. But none did it with more self-possession, style, grit, and black humor than *Dirty Harry*.

And no scene displayed that dark and "dirty" persona with more acuity than the film's bank robbery sequence in which Callahan, gun in hand, casually approaches a fallen thief who is reaching for his rifle. "Ah-ah," he chides the man, whose hand quivers just above the weapon. "I know what you're thinking: Did he fire six shots or only five?" In the brief lecture that follows, he extols the flesh-piercing merits of his Smith & Wesson .44 Magnum and challenges the man to blast his way free. "You've got to ask yourself one question," he growls. "Do I feel lucky? Well, do you, punk?"

When the robber backs down and asks Callahan, as an act of consolation, to tell him if there was a bullet left, Callahan calmly levels the piece at the man's horrified face and squeezes the trigger. It clicks hollowly on an empty chamber, and Callahan walks off chuckling. The same monologue was reprised dramatically in the final scene with considerably different results.

If there is a single moment with which Eastwood's career is identified, for better or worse, it is this one. For many, Clint Eastwood *is* Dirty Harry, and it is almost an exercise in absurdity to imagine any other actor uttering those lines. But surprisingly, it could have been Frank Sinatra. The original script had been purchased by Universal, which wanted Paul Newman in the title role. Newman declined on political principle, and the script was eventually sold to Warner Bros., where a deal was struck in which Irvin Kershner would produce and direct and Sinatra would star. But the production was set to begin in November 1970, when Ol' Blue Eyes injured his hand, and the part was offered to Eastwood.

At the time, Eastwood was primarily recognized as a star of violent Westerns, particularly Sergio Leone's 1960s "spaghetti" trilogy *(Fistful of Dollars; For a Few Dollars More;* and *The Good, the Bad, and the Ugly)* and *Hang 'Em High* in 1968. He had also recently starred in a number of pictures directed by legendary action director Don Siegel, and he agreed to play Dirty Harry on the condition that Siegel, who was under contract to Universal, would head the project. Warner Bros. consented and paid Universal for his services.

After ruling out New York (where the original script was set), and scouting Seattle as a possible loca-
tion, Siegel and Eastwood settled on San Francisco, where they were allowed to film in the mayor's office at City Hall. The shoot was physically grueling for the fifty-eight-year-old director, involving hikes up and down the city's steep streets and a number of helicopter and rooftop shots; Siegel has said he was surprised he didn't drop dead. At one point when he was laid up with the flu, Siegel allowed Eastwood to direct an important scene in which Callahan rescues a suicide jumper using a fire department crane—payback, perhaps, for Eastwood's casting of Siegel as a bartender in his directorial debut *Play Misty for Me,* which wrapped just before shooting on *Dirty Harry* began.

Such was the trust between the two men that when it came to the final scene, Siegel let Eastwood perform his own stunts—leaping onto a moving bus from a railroad trestle—and took his advice on the location, a rock quarry in Marin County that Eastwood remembered visiting as a child.

The final confrontation between Callahan and Scorpio occurs there. Cornered with his back to a pond, Scorpio grabs a young boy fishing nearby and holds a gun to his head, demanding that Callahan drop his weapon. Harry fires a shot, wounding Scorpio, and the child escapes.

Eastwood has said it was his idea to repeat the speech he made during the bank robbery, albeit with much less humor and a great deal more animosity—or "double pissed," as he has put it. It was a masterstroke. He hovers above the bleeding Scorpio, his anger boiling over, daring the killer to grab his gun with the line, "Well, do you, punk?!" Only this time, his enemy takes the bait, and Callahan blasts him into the water.

Knowing he has disobeyed orders from the chief of police and the mayor and frustrated by a system that would have let Scorpio escape, he takes out his shield. The script originally called for him to throw the badge into the water à la Gary Cooper in *High Noon*, but Eastwood felt the action was a bit hyperbolic. He con-

vinced Siegel to let him move as if to throw it, but draw back on second consideration. During filming, however, Eastwood changed his mind, and the movie ends with Callahan hurling the shield into the grimy water near Scorpio's floating corpse.

This finale, of course, implied the end of Dirty Harry's crime-fighting career, but that wasn't to be. The San Francisco Police Department's finest antihero was resurrected in 1973's *Magnum Force*, this time to battle—what else!—rogue cops bent on executing innocent but "undesirable" civilians. He returned three more times, in *The Enforcer* (1976), *Sudden Impact* (1983), and *The Dead Pool* (1988), honing the badass attitude that has influenced so many subsequent franchise per-

formances by other actors, from Bruce Willis in the *Die Hard* films to Mel Gibson in the *Lethal Weapon* series and Arnold Schwarzenegger in *The Terminator* movies.

Described by Siegel as a "wall-to-wall carpet of violence," the film played to packed houses beginning in late December 1971, eventually earning more than $22 million in domestic theatrical rentals for Warner Bros.

As if *Dirty Harry*'s worldwide appeal needed any confirmation, Andy Robinson, perhaps the unlikeliest of screen villains (the committed pacifist and vegetarian had to go through several weeks of training before he felt comfortable handling a rifle), says he still gets accosted wherever he goes by fans who demand: "Do you feel lucky? Well, do you, punk?"

TOUGH GUY MOMENTS

In addition to Dirty Harry, Clint Eastwood has played a fistful of other "tough guy" roles during his screen career. What makes a tough guy? A willingness to take a stand and a refusal to quit, no matter how bad the odds. And a modicum of charisma certainly helps. While Humphrey Bogart and Marlon Brando also qualify for inclusion on this list, they have their own lists in other chapters.

JOHN WAYNE in **Sands of Iwo Jima** (1949) Sergeant John M. Stryker (Wayne) and his men lie in the darkness listening to one of their own call for help. Stryker won't rescue the wounded man because it might expose the American forces to the Japanese. One rebellious grunt threatens to go, saying, "The only way you can stop me is to kill me," but Stryker doesn't back down. Although he's pained by his decision, he growls back, "That's just what I'll do. This mission is bigger than any individual." Heroism doesn't come easy.

GARY COOPER in **High Noon** (1952) The dialogue and acting are a bit stiff, but Cooper's character of Marshal Will Kane refuses to run from a showdown, even after the entire town abandons his cause. As he awaits the train's arrival, he is a man alone, facing his destiny as the clock ticks down.

JAMES DEAN in **Rebel Without a Cause** (1955) Don't call Jim Stark (Dean) chicken. To prove his manliness, Stark agrees to a challenge thrown at him by Buzz (Corey Allen)—a "chickie run," driving a car straight at a cliff and staying behind the wheel till the last possible minute. Don't try this at home.

SEAN CONNERY in **Dr. No** (1962) Our introduction to the man named "Bond, James Bond," comes at a glitzy casino, but he reveals his true 007 character while hiding from Dr. No's henchmen in the water with Honey Ryder (Ursula Andress). When one of the thugs discovers them, Bond quickly breaks his neck, killing him. A horrified Ryder asks why he did that, and Bond coolly replies, "Because I had to." Licensed to kill, indeed.

PAUL NEWMAN in **Cool Hand Luke** (1967) Luke (Newman) won't ever say uncle. He keeps coming back for more in a brutal boxing match–turned–beating against Dragline (George Kennedy), and he proves his mettle by eating fifty eggs in one hour without losing his grin. Finally, with guns trained on him after an escape attempt, he sasses back to a prison captain (Strother Martin), mocking the captain's famous line "What we've got here is a failure to communicate."

CHARLTON HESTON in **Planet of the Apes** (1968). George Taylor (Heston) is stranded in the future on a planet controlled by dictatorial apes; humans cannot speak and are treated as slaves. Taylor has been temporarily rendered mute, and he attempts to escape. He is soon caught in a net like a beast, but he finds his voice again with his defiant response: "Get your stinking paws off me, you damn dirty ape."

STEVE MCQUEEN in **Papillon** (1973). McQueen's Henri "Papillon" Charriere is falsely imprisoned and determined to escape from a notorious prison in French Guyana. He shows how far a man can bend without breaking. Already in solitary confinement, Papillon is choked by a guard and threatened with half rations during an interrogation, but he still refuses to rat on a friend. "I was born skinny," he snarls back.

MEL GIBSON in **Mad Max** (1979). Max Rockatansky (Gibson) wants to quit the police force before he becomes just like the "terminal crazies" he chases down. When his wife and child are attacked, Max turns vigilante. He ankle-cuffs bad guy Johnny (Tim Burns) to an over-turned truck, lights a fuse that will blow the truck up, and gives Johnny a hacksaw telling him it'll take too long to cut through the handcuffs, but "if you're lucky you can hack through the ankle in five minutes." Then he rides off into the sunset.

KEANU REEVES in **The Matrix** (1999). Some heroes are born tough; some have tough-ness thrust upon them. Thomas Anderson (Reeves) is a corporate grunt by day but an obsessed computer hacker nicknamed Neo by night. Then he's told he is the Chosen One destined to save humanity from slavery to machines. In the lengthy final battle, evil Agent Smith (Hugo Weaving) headlocks him before an oncoming train, saying, "Good-bye, Mr. Anderson," but Neo responds, "My name . . . is Neo" and bursts free at the last second. Of course, freezing a barrage of bullets in midair is pretty impressive, too.

THE EXORCIST

1973

Decades after its release, *The Exorcist* still ranks among the most terrifying movies ever made. Although the kind of special effects artistry employed to make the demonic possession believable has been refined immensely since 1973, the film still shocks and dismays. Perhaps it's the movie's factual underpinnings that lend it an air of credibility—a believability that makes it more than a simple horror film.

The Exorcist was based on the 1971 best-selling horror novel by William Peter Blatty, inspired by an actual event that caught Blatty's attention while attending Georgetown University in January 1949. It involved the only known occurrence of an exorcism in the United States—the three-month torment of a fourteen-year-old boy in Mt. Rainier, Maryland.

Twenty years after the events, Blatty was able to convince a publishing company that his proposed book was viable. In doing research, he learned that one of the priests involved in the exorcism had kept a diary, but before he would allow Blatty access, the writer had to promise to disguise the original case. After Blatty offered to change the possessed child from a fourteen-year-old boy to a twelve-year-old girl, the priest let him see his diary, and Blatty incorporated it into his book.

When the novel *The Exorcist* finally came out, it was a huge best-seller—the book "everybody" was reading—and the stage was set for the film. When the book was optioned for the movies, Blatty wrote the screenplay.

Like all great movies, *The Exorcist* was a collaboration with all the elements contributing to its success. And though the acting, script, photography, and special effects are all first-rate, the director, William Friedkin, who'd won the Best Director Oscar for *The French Connection*, says the movie would not have been as effective without its amazing sound. It was the sound that set the mood and "sold" the film's reality.

The spellbinding melody "Tubular Bells" by Mike Oldfield was key, but more important was the sound of the demon inhabiting Regan MacNeil's body. When the film was shot, thirteen-year-old Linda Blair, who had been acting and modeling since she was six, was chosen out of six hundred candidates to play the possessed child. Blair actually spoke every line of her demonic dialogue. Then it was rerecorded by voice actor Ken Nordine, and the sound engineers combined his voice with Blair's. Even after they employed such recording tricks as distortion, echo, and over-amplification, Friedkin was disappointed. He said it sounded like a man's voice coming out of a child's face. He needed an otherworldly voice that was neither male nor female. After agonizing over the problem, a name popped into his head: Mercedes McCambridge, a smoky-voiced movie actress who had also worked in radio with broadcast great Orson Welles.

Friedkin found McCambridge, then in her fifties, working in Texas, and flew her to Hollywood. After watching a rough cut of the movie, she agreed to take on the monumental task. It took three weeks for McCambridge to produce the demonic sounds. "She made wheezing sounds akin to what you can imagine a person inhabited by various demons would sound like," Friedkin says. "It was pure inspiration."

Even with the director's endorsement, it wasn't until McCambridge engaged in a legal battle with Warner Bros. that she was finally given the credit for providing the voice of the demon.

Of course, accompanying those horrifying voices were state-of-the-art special effects. Among the torments inflicted upon Blair were techniques that set new standards for creepiness. As the demon dragged poor

Regan further and further into his clutches, the disturbing special effects grew more and more repulsive.

When a skeptical Father Damien Karras, played by first-time actor and award-winning playwright Jason Miller, pays his initial visit to Regan, the action ratchets up. As Karras and Karl, the MacNeils' houseman (played by Rudolf Schündler), grimly climb the stairs, they hear unearthly, horrific sounds escaping from Regan's room. Karl explains, "It wants no straps."

Father Karras opens the door, and there in front of him is a terrifying sight: the child/demon straining at the straps that bind her to her four-poster bed, her face discolored and slashed, her wild eyes a satanic yellowish brown, her hair filthy and matted, a breathing tube coming from her nostril. Karras gathers his courage and says, "Hello, Regan. I'm a friend of your mother's. I'd like to help you. I'm Damien Karras."

Out of the possessed twelve-year-old comes a growling, gravelly, centuries-old voice from the bowels of hell: "And I'm the devil. Now kindly undo these straps!"

Taunting the demon, Karras challenges back, "If you're the devil, why not make the straps disappear?"

Regan arrogantly retorts, "That's much too vulgar a display of power, Karras."

The conversation grows ever more tense when Regan spitefully informs Father Karras that his recently deceased mother "is in here with us. . . . Would you like to leave a message? I'll see that she gets it."

"If that's true," Karras challenges, "then you must know my mother's maiden name. What is it?" He stands, walks to the bed, and asks again, "What is it?"

Right then, the priest gets an answer that he and the audience are quite unprepared for. As he leans in, Regan lurches upright and projectile vomits a torrent of thick green goo in Karras's face. The gelatinous gunk sticks to his face and clothes and to Regan's nightshirt.

What looks like a gush of underworld slime was actually garden-variety pea soup, and it wasn't coming from Linda Blair's throat. Makeup artist Dick Smith felt the rig that pumped the soup was too demanding for the young actress. So the apparatus that spewed the vile green concoction was strapped to stuntwoman Eileen Dietz, who was made up to look like Blair.

The film's most horrifying and memorable

moments come during the scenes of the actual exorcism in Regan's room. Father Karras is joined by Father Lankester Merrin, an elderly and scholarly Jesuit Catholic priest played by legendary Swedish actor Max von Sydow.

In order to visually create the freezing temperatures generally thought to accompany ghostly presence, the set for Regan's bedroom was built on a refrigerated soundstage in New York City, where all the film's interiors were shot. The filmmakers were able to chill the set down to twenty degrees below zero, making the actors' breath visible and enabling them to convincingly shiver from both cold and fright.

Once the ritual begins, the demon telekinetically causes the room to quake violently, the furniture to move across the floor, and Regan's bed to shake fiercely. What is probably the most disconcerting shot in the movie is when Regan's head turns 360 degrees.

Makeup wizard Dick Smith accomplished the effect by placing a mask of Linda Blair's face on a mannequin rigged so that frozen "breath" emerged from its mouth as the head spun.

The tossing furniture and spinning head are followed by the relatively serene yet just as startling spectacle of Regan's eyes rolling back in her head and her body suddenly "levitating" over her four-poster bed. Blair was rigged with painted wires that were fed through tiny holes in the ceiling and moved up and down by electric motors to produce this haunting piece of movie magic.

Despite tepid reviews (the *New York Times* called it "a chunk of elegant occultist claptrap"), *The Exorcist* packed theaters when it opened in December 1973. Some theaters reported audience members being so frightened they became ill or fled the theater during certain parts of the movie.

However, when Oscar time came, *The Exorcist* was presented with ten Academy Award nominations: Best Picture, Best Actress (Ellen Burstyn), Best Supporting Actor (Jason Miller), Best Supporting Actress (Linda Blair), Best Director (William Friedkin), Best Adapted Screenplay (William Peter Blatty), Best Cinematography (Owen Roizman), Best Art Direction/Set Decoration (Bill Malley and Jerry Wunderlich), Best Sound (Robert Knudson and Chris Newman), and Best Film Editing (Jordan Leondopoulos, Bud Smith, Evan Lottman, and Norman Gay). Blatty won the Oscar for his screenplay and Knudson and Newman for their sound work.

The Exorcist transformed the horror genre, giving it credibility and lifting it beyond its lowbrow, low-budget roots to reach a huge mainstream audience. It is to the filmmakers' everlasting credit that, years after *The Exorcist* first horrified moviegoers all over the world, it still possesses the power to frighten, captivate, and entertain.

HORROR MOMENTS

When it comes to telling terrifying tales, the milieu of a darkened theater has always given the movies an advantage over other methods of storytelling. Here are horror scenes of recent vintage that became big box office successes by scaring audiences to the edge of their seats.

The Omen (1976) Long overshadowed by *The Exorcist*, this is a haunting devil-possession movie in its own right, stylishly directed by Richard Donner and featuring strong performances from Gregory Peck and Lee Remick as the Thorns, whose child, Damien, turns out to be the anti-Christ.

There are numerous indelible scares along the way. The most gory and notorious is the decapitation of photographer Keith Jennings (David Warner). The most shocking is the first jolt when Damien's nanny climbs to the roof during a party and shouts "Look at me, Damien" before plunging off with a noose around her neck, shattering the glass windows and the Thorns' idyllic world. The most imaginative moment is the zoo scene when the baboons, instinctively understanding Damien's nature, attack the car carrying him and his mother. (A zookeeper actually sat in the backseat with the alpha baboon to make the baboons go crazy.)

Halloween (1978) Director John Carpenter's low-budget horror film shows restraint early on, scaring viewers with shots filmed from the viewpoint of escaped psychopath Michael Myers (Nick Castle) and by displaying the mounting fear of spooked-out Laurie (Jamie Lee Curtis), the terrorized teen. When the killing starts in earnest, it feels less gratuitous than the violence in the myriad sequels and imitators that followed. More frightening than Michael's murders is the final moment after Laurie stabs Michael three times, and the hero Dr. Loomis (Donald Pleasance) shoots him six times and sees him fall from a second-floor balcony. When Dr. Loomis looks down, however, Michael is gone, having disappeared into the night.

Scream (1996) As the movie that revived the horror genre, *Scream* simultaneously flaunted and parodied slasher-movie conventions. A killer is on the loose and Sidney Prescott (Neve Campbell) and her high school pals are the main targets. The plot is basic because it deliberately follows the genre's formulas.

The most nerve-racking scene is actually the twelve-minute opener in which Casey Becker (Drew Barrymore) is home alone making popcorn when she gets a threatening phone call. The caller toys with her and with the audience, peppering her with threats and with trivia questions about horror movies that she must answer to save both herself and her captured boyfriend. The nail-biting scene prompts plenty of nervous laughter, especially since audiences presume a star like Barrymore will survive. Screams of terror are quickly replaced by screams of horror as Casey is slaughtered while her parents accidentally eavesdrop.

The Blair Witch Project (1999) Terrifying in its simplicity, this movie is a fake documentary about young filmmakers hunting a mythological witch in the forest. The actors really lived in the woods for days while the directors scared them, heightening the raw, genuine quality of the acting. There is little gore and we never see the witch, which also heightens the tension and perfectly captures our fear of the unknown. While Heather's flashlight confessional is the most famous scene, it isn't the scariest. When the documentary crew's cameras are off, the audience sees a black screen, hearing only the increasingly hysterical voices of the filmmakers. When Heather (Heather Donohue) and Michael (Michael Williams) plunge into the night screaming for their missing friend Josh (Josh Leonard), their fear is palpable and their cries go right through you.

THE GODFATHER PART II

1974

The annals of organized crime in America brim with colorful, ruthless personalities bent on protecting their "family" empires. The crooked antics of mobsters from Al Capone to John Gotti have been splashed across the nation's papers and eagerly reported on the nightly news, feeding the public's never-ending appetite for intrigue, betrayal, violence, and, occasionally, redemption.

Yet perhaps the country's best-known and most celebrated mob saga of all didn't play out in a federal courtroom or on the streets of New York, Chicago, or Las Vegas, but on the big screen. Francis Ford Coppola's hugely successful *Godfather* films, which traced the tragic arc of the fictional Corleone crime family,

defined for many the character of the "Mafia don" and today stand collectively as one of the great achievements in American cinematic history.

The Godfather (1972), based on Mario Puzo's best-selling 1969 novel and starring Marlon Brando, Al Pacino, Robert Duvall, and James Caan, told the story of Michael Corleone's assumption of power after the death of his crime-boss father, Vito, and his subsequent war on the family's enemies during the 1940s and early 1950s. It was Coppola's first high-profile effort, and the film became an unexpected sensation, collecting ten Academy Award nominations and becoming the highest-grossing movie in history at the time, with nearly $82 million in box office receipts in 1972 alone.

Naturally, Paramount wanted to capitalize on the success, and a mere four months after the release of *The Godfather,* the studio announced that a sequel was in the works. But what appeared to be a well-oiled commercial juggernaut was, in fact, a wheezing jalopy of acrimony, bitterness, and bruised egos. Despite the film's phenomenal reception, Coppola's experience

making *The Godfather* had left a bad taste in his mouth; studio executives had fought the young director every step of the way, from his initial decision to cast Marlon Brando and then-unknown Al Pacino in the title roles to his editing of the final product. Constantly afraid of being fired and replaced midfilm, the thirty-two-year-old Coppola had to request sleeping pills from the studio's physician for his stress-related insomnia.

The idea that there would, or could, ever be a second *Godfather* film struck Coppola as tacky, and he jokingly vowed that the only sequel he would make would be *Abbott & Costello Meet the Godfather.* But cash is the salve for many wounds, and when Paramount offered Coppola $500,000 to cowrite, direct, and produce the $11 million film, as well as an unprecedented 13 percent of the adjusted gross and complete directorial control, a deal was made.

The massive production, which included hundreds of extras and large, lavish sets, was filmed over a nine-month period during 1973 and 1974 in New York; Miami; Lake Tahoe; Trieste, Sicily; and the Dominican Republic. Like the first movie, *The Godfather Part II* was cowritten by Puzo and Coppola. But it was more ambitious in concept and broader in scope than the original, spanning six decades and two distinct story lines. The first story picks up in the late 1950s, several years after the close of *The Godfather,* as Michael Corleone (Pacino) attempts to expand the family's criminal influence in Las Vegas and Cuba while facing down his rivals and his enemies within the ranks. The second story travels back in time to portray the rise to prominence of the young Sicilian godfather Vito Corleone (played by Brando in the first film and Robert De Niro in the second) in New York's Little Italy in the 1910s and 1920s.

Coppola envisioned *The Godfather Part II* less as a sequel and more of a companion piece to the first film, one that would amplify and explore the themes of loyalty, family, and power broached in the earlier production. Nowhere is the tragic intersection of these elements more evident than in Pacino's hard-edged portrayal of Michael, who somewhat reluctantly took the reins of family power but allowed that power to corrupt his relationships. It is a tragedy made all the more poignant by the juxtaposition of parallel scenes of

Vito Corleone's youthful optimism and dogged efforts to protect his family.

One of the film's most unforgettable moments is the gut-wrenching scene in which Michael—isolated, brooding, and increasingly ruthless after several botched deals, a Senate investigation, and an assassination attempt—turns on his somewhat dim-witted older brother Fredo (John Cazale) for the latter's disloyalty. In the midst of New Year's revelry and chaos, Michael plants the symbolic "kiss of death" on Fredo, revealing to him that he's aware of his traitorous actions. After Fredo, in a fit of near apoplexy, pleads that he was unwittingly led astray by the family's enemies, Michael pronounces sentence on him in the chilling, emotionless manner that has come to mark his evolution from benign protector to Machiavellian dictator. "You're nothing to me now," he tells Fredo in a near whisper. "You're not a brother; you're not a friend. I don't want to know you or what you do. I don't want to see you at the hotels; I don't want you near my house. When you see our mother, I want to know a day in advance so I won't be there." Upon exiting the room, Michael informs one of his henchmen in cryptic but no uncertain terms that Fredo is to be executed once the brothers' mother passes away.

This "excommunication" sequence, which Coppola considered among the best in the film, represents the spiritual crux of the story, for it marks the moment at which the schism between Michael's love for his family and his desire for absolute power becomes irreparable. It was, however, a matter of some contention between Coppola and Puzo.

Coppola thought it necessary for Michael to have Fredo murdered immediately in order to pound home the thematic point, while Puzo argued that despite Michael's transformation, he would never have his own brother whacked. The two eventually settled on a script that had Michael holding off on his plans for the sake of the Corleone matriarch. During the penultimate scene, an operatic montage of vengeance and violence in which, one by one, Michael's enemies are knocked off, the seemingly unsuspecting Fredo takes a bullet to the head while fishing outside the family's compound on Lake Tahoe.

With a hefty running time of nearly three and a half hours, *The Godfather Part II* opened in December 1974 to mixed reviews. A critic at one New York paper referred to the film as "fairly lame," calling it a "Frankenstein's monster" cobbled together from leftover parts of the original. Another New York review lauded the picture as "a modern American epic" and Coppola as a "major artist."

Audiences' initial reactions varied as well, but the film had a good first weekend, due in part to the fact that NBC television had paid a whopping $10 million to broadcast the original *Godfather*, with Coppola as host, just prior to the sequel's release. The airing attracted ninety million viewers, the fourth-largest audience for a movie in television history.

The Godfather Part II went on to earn a not-insubstantial $57.3 million that year, still something of a disappointment to the studio brass, who had predicted a *Godfather*-like box office performance.

While *The Godfather Part II* did not equal the initial commercial success of the first film, the quality of its performances could not be overlooked, and the initial lukewarm reception gradually grew into a chorus of tribute. When the Academy Awards rolled around, *The Godfather Part II* racked up eleven nominations, surpassing *The Godfather* in 1972, and took home six.

Four actors—Michael V. Gazzo, as the Corleone ally-turned-enemy Frank Pentangeli; Lee Strasberg, as the Meyer Lansky–inspired gangster Hyman Roth; Talia Shire, as Connie Corleone; and Robert De Niro, as the young Vito—were nominated for their supporting roles. De Niro, who spent time in Sicily and worked with a Sicilian dialect coach in preparation for his part, took home the statue, one of only four actors in history to earn the honor for a performance in a foreign language.

Oscar honors also went to Dean Tavoularis, Angelo Graham, and George R. Nelson for Art Direction and

composers Nino Rota and Carmine Coppola (the director's father) for Original Dramatic Score. Pacino was duly honored with a nomination for Best Actor, but was edged out by Art Carney for his role in *Harry and Tonto.* Coppola himself mounted the stage three times to receive awards for Best Screenplay, Best Director, and Best Picture (a category in which, interestingly enough, he competed against himself for his work on *The Conversation,* starring Gene Hackman). *The Godfather Part II* was the only sequel in film history to walk away with a Best Picture honor.

If *The Godfather* had earned Coppola a spot in Hollywood as a major player, *The Godfather Part II* cemented his growing reputation as a consummate auteur willing to take big chances with big money. Sixteen years later, Coppola, Pacino, and Shire regrouped to make *The Godfather Part III,* adding to the success of the first two. All told, the *Godfather* trilogy amassed twenty-eight Academy Award nominations and earned nearly $260 million at the box office, making it one of the most successful franchises in movie history and the high-water mark for crime epics.

GANGSTER MOMENTS

Since the earliest days of motion pictures, the drama, violence, and larger-than-life characters of the criminal underworld have been glorified by the movies. Long before the epic trilogy that presented the Corleone crime family as tragic heroes in pursuit of the American dream, mob films were usually low-budget cops-and-robbers shoot-'em-ups filled with car chases and tommy-gun battles. Here are five standouts in the gangster genre.

Little Caesar (1930) The first classic gangster movie featured one of the ultimate bad guys, Edward G. Robinson, as Rico "Little Caesar" Bandello. Rico trusts no one and after taking over a gang, he threatens them with the sort of dialogue that would be imitated by film noir writers for decades to come: "There's a rope around my neck right now, and they only hang ya once. If anybody turns yella and squeals, my gun's gonna speak its piece."

Public Enemy (1931) Hot on the heels of *Little Caesar*, this film was even grittier and tougher, making a superstar of James Cagney as Tom Powers. Powers is a swaggering bantam throughout, but his most memorable scene came during a breakfast argument with his mistress, Kitty (Mae Clarke). Fed up with her behavior, Powers sneers, "I wish you was a wishing well, so that I could tie a bucket to ya and sink ya." Then he stuffs a half grapefruit in her face. Now that's being tough.

Scarface (1983) Al Pacino's performance as Michael Corleone was brilliant for its understated restraint. In *Scarface*, a much bolder, less subtle film (it was, after all, directed by Brian De Palma and written by Oliver Stone), Pacino made every moment as Tony Montana count by going over the top—way over. The film's zenith is its finale when Tony stands at the top of his staircase, shouts, "Say hello to my leetle friend," and unleashes a frenzy of firepower while absorbing a hail of bullets in his cocaine-fueled body.

Goodfellas (1990) When the volatile Tommy DeVito (Joe Pesci) commits the Mafia's carnal sin of murdering a "made man" in a rage, he and fellow mobsters Jimmy Conway (Robert De Niro) and Henry Hill (Ray Liotta) must drive the body upstate to bury it. First they sneak into Tommy's house to get a knife and a shovel. Even though it's the middle of the night, Tommy's mama comes in and insists on cooking a good Italian meal for them. Her blind acceptance of Tommy's ludicrous explanation for the blood on his shirt and his need for the knife and shovel—they ran over a deer and need to pry the hoof off the grill—is not only unnervingly funny but also pathetic, demonstrating just how skewed everyone's perspectives and values are. The trio subsequently are shocked to learn that the man in the trunk is not dead. Tommy plunges his mother's knife into the body several more times and Jimmy fires a few rounds into it. Then even Henry begins to realize that he needs to leave the mob world behind.

Bugsy (1991) In a richly textured portrait of a complex man, Warren Beatty captures both the brutality and glamour of Benjamin "Bugsy" Siegel's world. Siegel was a visionary businessman who helped launch Las Vegas, but he was also a psychopath. His different sides come together when he realizes Jack Dragna (Richard Sarafian) has been skimming money. In a savage scene, he threatens to kill Dragna but instead humiliates him by making him crawl on the floor and bark like a dog. Dragna actually feels grateful when he leaves, and Siegel sits down and begins hungrily shoving food into his mouth. He's interrupted by his new paramour, Virginia Hill (Annette Bening), who is so turned on by Siegel's sadistic side that she throws herself at him in the scene's climax.

JAWS

1975

In 1974, Steven Spielberg was a twenty-seven-year-old director with one theatrical release to his credit, *The Sugarland Express,* when he set out to make a movie based on the best-selling Peter Benchley novel *Jaws,* the tale of a fictional coastal resort town terrorized by a man-eating great white shark. The experience was nightmarish for both audiences and Spielberg, but for decidedly different reasons.

From its horrifying opening sequence showing a helpless swimmer being violently thrashed about and devoured by an unseen predator to the shockingly explosive ending, *Jaws* struck a frightening and visceral chord with moviegoers. The tensely paced thriller attracted audiences in droves, quickly making it the first-ever $100 million box office hit. For Spielberg and company, the making of *Jaws* was a frustrating, laborious experience that tested their patience and endurance. The production became so legendary for its problems that the crew nicknamed it *Flaws.*

The problems presented themselves almost immediately when casting quandaries lingered until just two weeks before shooting began in May 1974. The three main roles were the town's principled police chief Martin Brody, a bearded and bespectacled ichthyologist Matt Hooper, and Peter Quint, a "salty" World War II vet turned shark hunter.

Jon Voight turned down the role of Hooper and so did Richard Dreyfuss. But *Jaws* screenwriter Carl Gottlieb, an old friend of Dreyfuss's, persuaded Dreyfuss to reconsider. Charlton Heston wanted to play Brody, but Spielberg offered the role to Robert Duvall instead. But Duvall lost out altogether when he told Spielberg that he preferred to play Quint, a part the director had already offered first to Lee Marvin and then to Sterling Hayden. Finally, Robert Shaw was enlisted as Quint and Roy Scheider was given the role of Brody. (Shaw

form stunts with dummies, and Spielberg could shoot from inside a shark cage. They soon realized that there is no such thing as a trained great white.

So Zanuck and Brown reeled in special effects pioneer Bob Mattey out of retirement to build a mechanical shark. Mattey had built rocket ships for *Flash Gordon* and a fifteen-foot mechanical alligator for

not only contributed great acting, he was also responsible for much of Quint's memorable tale about surviving the sharks surrounding the USS *Indianapolis* during World War II.)

With casting complete, the filmmaker's biggest challenges were still yet to come. Even though movies about the sea had traditionally been shot in large water tanks on studio back lots, Spielberg wanted the realism he could get only by shooting at sea. Producers Richard Zanuck and David Brown agreed, blithely presuming someone could train a great white shark to per-

Tarzan, and he masterminded the effects for *20,000 Leagues Under the Sea.* But even before Mattey could get his mechanical mashers ready for filming, the movie ran into its first near-disaster.

Seeking ultimate authenticity, Spielberg hired documentary filmmakers to shoot real shark footage in Australia. Warned that most great whites were more like fourteen feet rather than the twenty-five-foot monster of the film, Spielberg had a shark cage built five-eighths the regular size, then hired Carl Rizzo, a four-foot-nine stuntman, to make the shark loom larger.

The first time Rizzo descended in the cage, a shark closed in. Rizzo panicked, lost his scuba air regulator, and had to be pulled up. On the next attempt, the shark's performance was almost too realistic. Before Rizzo could even get in the water, the shark attacked, producing extraordinary underwater footage, becoming some of the film's most shocking images.

While Mattey and his assistants were still in Hollywood building the three three-thousand-pound hydraulically operated sharks, Spielberg began working around the shark's absence while shooting on Martha's Vineyard. He had chosen Martha's Vineyard because it

required cash bribes to depart, and others lingered in hostile rebellion.

Another scene shot in the chilly coastal waters was the movie's opening sequence, perhaps its most terrifying and memorable. The audience witnesses the ferocious nature of the great white without ever actually seeing the shark. The scene begins with a view of the dangerous undersea world from the predator's viewpoint as it searches for food. Enhancing the tension is composer John Williams's ominous two-note (E and F) "da-dum" theme music (performed on a cello and a bass). Spielberg originally rejected this score, telling

was the only location where he could be out at sea with a sandy bottom only thirty feet down, which was necessary for the shark's crane equipment.

But the weather was uncooperative; the waters were extremely cold for filming the beach scenes, and the delays meant that boating season was in full swing just when Spielberg was trying to film scenes showing Quint's shark-hunting vessel, the *Orca*, isolated at sea. Passing ships constantly interrupted filming; some

Williams he preferred something more melodic and less primitive, but Williams argued that the notes symbolized the shark's mindless instincts, winning Spielberg over and later earning Williams an Oscar for Best Score.

The scene cuts to a teenage beach party. A blonde named Christine "Chrissie" Watkins, played by twenty-seven-year-old stuntwoman Susan Backlinie, announces she's going for a swim. As she runs to the water, stripping en route, a drunken boy eager for a late-night skinny-dip chases her to the shore. The boy struggles to get his clothes off, takes a tumble, then passes out on the beach while Chrissie frolics in the water.

Suddenly, Chrissie is violently yanked under the surface and then brutally dragged from side to side by the unseen underwater predator. Her horrified screams of "God, help me!" go unnoticed. Her struggle ends when she's jerked under for the final time, devoured. The water is quiet again.

To capture the terror, cinematographer Bill Butler reconfigured the camera boxes so Spielberg could shoot the scene, and much of the movie, with the camera at water level. Backlinie was fitted with specially

rigged underwater pants. Cables attached to the stomach and thigh panels of the pants ran to a diver below her in the water and to crewmembers on the sand. The diver pulled one cable to make Backlinie jerk under the water and then the crew on the sand would run from side to side tugging the other cables to make her body flail about.

In spite of his creative devices, Spielberg ultimately had to have a shark appear. Mattey's sharks (one named "Bruce" after Spielberg's attorney) were built to dive, surface, chew, and travel seventy feet. Unfortunately, the three models, priced at $250,000 each, never matched the power of their live counterparts.

On the first day of filming with the mechanical sharks, one immediately sank into Nantucket Sound. When the crew recovered it and got it moving properly, the compressed air in the machine's hydraulic system exploded.

The mishap inspired the movie's climactic scene in which Brody shoves a tank of compressed air in the shark's mouth, then tauntingly shouts, "Smile, you son of a bitch!" as he shoots the tank and blows the shark to bits. Spielberg's idea of blowing up the shark was a major source of conflict with author Peter Benchley, who deemed it unrealistic and over the top.

The director confidently assured Benchley that if he grabbed the audience in the first two hours, he could do whatever he wanted in the last three minutes. "And I want the audience on their feet screaming," Spielberg added. It produced both Spielberg's desired catharsis and one of the film's most memorable lines. Brody's other famous line, "You're gonna need a bigger boat," was uttered when he got his first unwanted close-up view of the shark.

The team of underwater scuba technicians had trouble coordinating the mechanical shark's actions—one day his eyes would cross, the next his jaws wouldn't close properly. Then Spielberg discovered the shark's neoprene foam flesh hadn't been tested in saltwater, and the skin was dissolving to reveal the machinery beneath.

Again, Spielberg responded to adversity with imagination, filming fewer shark shots and instead building suspense and fear by employing ingenious Hitchcock-ian techniques, such as signifying the shark's presence by showing only a fin tearing through the water's surface and filming the bobbing yellow barrels attached to the shark by Quint's harpoon. Spielberg conferred menace onto once harmless items, leaving viewers unable to see the true danger. "Those barrels really saved us," producer Zanuck has said.

But for Quint's death and the nail-biting climax, Spielberg had to have the shark lunge out of the water and onto the boat forcefully and frighteningly. In the book and early scripts, Quint—like Ahab of *Moby-Dick*—went over the side and drowned after getting his leg caught while trying for an up-close harpooning. Spielberg decided the movie needed a bigger jolt and wanted the shark to attack the boat and consume the obsessed hunter.

Unfortunately, Bob Mattey's shark failed to perform once again. One production executive described

the first take as looking like "a dolphin walking along the water and falling on the boat." Ultimately, Spielberg and Verna Fields, who won the Oscar for Best Editing on *Jaws*, were forced to patch together the shark's attack and subsequent devouring of Quint with quick cuts in the editing room.

By August 1974, the film was approaching one hundred days over schedule, and the original $4 million budget had more than doubled. After weeks on the boats, the cast and crew were close to breaking down or rebelling. To cope with the tedium, Shaw admitted, "I tend to drink when totally bored—scotch, vodka, gin, whatever." He also amused himself by abusing Dreyfuss, making anti-Semitic remarks and chiding him for talking "interminably." Dreyfuss admits that Shaw, a nice guy in private and a terror in public, pushed his buttons. "If any of us had any sense," Dreyfuss once famously stated, "we'd all bail out now."

Spielberg learned that, as an expression of their frustration and to celebrate the last day of shooting, the cast and crew were planning to throw him overboard. One last time, however, he outsmarted trouble: He prepared the final shot, but before it was filmed, he jumped into a waiting boat and sped off to safety. His final triumphant words as he departed from Martha's Vineyard were, "I shall not return."

Jaws premiered on June 20, 1975, and eleven weeks later it surpassed *The Godfather* as the highest-grossing film of its day. In the aftermath of its extraordinary success, *Jaws* chased people from the beaches with its "Don't go in the water" slogan, landed on the cover of *Time* magazine, and spawned three sequels.

Along with *Star Wars* two years later, *Jaws* prompted movie studios to lavish their budgets on expensive, effects-driven action-adventure films, betting their bottom line on summer blockbusters.

Unforgettable
ANIMAL MOMENTS

"Man against beast" has been a popular theme throughout Hollywood's history. Here are some of the more memorable terrifying moments.

King Kong (1933 and 1976) A gigantic ape captured on a remote island is brought back to New York for exhibition. This classic precursor of effects-driven movies is filled with unforgettable moments, including Kong's battle with a pterodactyl, the beauty held captive in his giant palm, and his last stance against the aircraft encircling and shooting at him as he makes his desperate climb up the Empire State Building.

The Birds (1963) What makes Alfred Hitchcock's adaptation of Daphne Du Maurier's 1952 short story so terrifying is the idea that such a common, shy animal could suddenly and inexplicably turn so frighteningly aggressive. This Hitchcock classic about a Northern California town suddenly under siege by thousands of attacking birds had everyone warily looking toward the sky.

Willard (1971 and 2003) Willard is a peculiar sort who's tormented by constant ridicule from his coworkers. His only friends are a couple of pet rats. When one of his beloved rats is killed, Willard is driven over the brink of sanity. With the help of Ben, his remaining pet rat, Willard exacts revenge on his coworkers by recruiting and unleashing an army of bloodthirsty rats.

Cujo (1983) Adapted from the Stephen King novel, this horror-thriller tells the terrifying tale of how a bite from a rabid bat turns Cujo, the Camber family's lovable St. Bernard, into a killer. When Donna Trenton (Dee Wallace-Stone) and her son, Tad (Danny Pintauro), take her car to Joe Camber's garage for repairs, they're helplessly trapped for hours by the rampaging monstrous dog.

ROCKY

1976

Life was imitating art at the 1976 Academy Award ceremonies. Sylvester Stallone stood triumphantly center stage, having risen from obscurity, gone the distance by Hollywood standards, and joined heavyweights Charlie Chaplin *(The Great Dictator)* and Orson Welles *(Citizen Kane)* as the only performers simultaneously nominated for Best Actor and Best Original Screenplay. Although he lost both, his movie *Rocky* won Best Picture, a crowning achievement for a writer-actor who, like the fighter in his movie, was given "a million-to-one shot."

While the story was hardly original, it stood out in 1976 because of its stark contrast to the decade's spate of disaffected, antihero films that reflected American society in turmoil like *Taxi Driver, Dog Day Afternoon,* and *Serpico. Rocky* opened Hollywood's eyes in a post-Nixon, post-Vietnam America craving a different outlook.

Just like his movie's working-class hero, writer-actor Michael Sylvester Enzio Stallone had a rough start. The drooping lip and eyelids that were part of Rocky's charm were caused by facial nerve damage during Stallone's birth. His parents offered little encouragement: Stallone's father originally delivered the line Rocky attributes to *his* father, "You weren't born with much of a brain, so you'd better develop your body."

As a struggling actor, Stallone was stuck in roles off-off-Broadway and in soft-core porn while working day jobs such as cleaning the lions' cages in the Central Park Zoo. Stallone got his break in the 1974 film *The Lords of Flatbush*. To pursue more movie work, Stallone, along with his then-wife, Sasha, and their bull-mastiff, Butkus, drove to Hollywood. Although he sold a few television scripts, his acting career stalled.

But in 1975, Stallone's life changed forever after watching Chuck Wepner, a mediocre New Jersey club boxer derided as the "Bayonne Bleeder," knock down and nearly go the distance with Muhammad Ali. Inspired by Wepner's courage and determination, Stallone began feverishly writing a screenplay in longhand, cranking out

a ninety-page script in only three days. His first version of *Rocky* was a dark movie featuring a bitter Balboa as an antihero who throws the big fight in the end to escape the dirty world that has ensnared him. Stallone later said that only 10 percent of the original script survived.

After his wife voiced her dislike for the character's disheartened nature, Stallone rewrote *Rocky* as a "never-say-die" underdog like himself, but his strong identification with the character almost derailed the film. Producers Irwin Winkler and Robert Chartoff, along with United Artists studio executives, wanted a big star—Ryan O'Neal, James Caan, or Burt Reynolds—for the title role.

They tried buying Stallone out, but he believed this was his one chance, the role he was born to play. With only about one hundred dollars to his name, Stallone resolutely refused each offer, even when they soared past a quarter of a million dollars. The studio grudgingly acquiesced, but without a major star slashed the

movie's budget from $1.7 million to $1 million, making the producers promise to personally cover budget overruns and paying Stallone a mere $25,000. Fortunately, Stallone's deal included 10 percent of the profits, which ultimately earned him millions of dollars.

Once *Rocky* was given the green light, the rest of the cast was put in place. Originally, Lee Strasberg was cast in the role of Mickey, Rocky's aging, tough-talking trainer, and boxer Ken Norton was to play champion Apollo Creed. But Strasberg wanted too much money and Norton bailed right before filming began in order to participate in a television superstar competition. Actors Burgess Meredith replaced Strasberg and Carl Weathers replaced Norton. Actress Talia Shire was also signed at the last minute to play Adrian, Rocky's love interest.

The movie was shot in just twenty-eight days and everyone pitched in: Producer Irwin Winkler's office became Creed's; the production manager doubled as a bum who Rocky carried into a bar; Stallone's wife took the still photographs; his brother, Frank, appeared as a street singer; and his father, Frank Sr., rang the bell during the fight scenes.

Despite the team effort, the undersized budget caused problems. All of the interior scenes for the movie were shot in Los Angeles. Rocky's apartment was in a smelly, dingy flophouse that was perfect—except for the palm trees outside the window. So the crew put up a brick wall, making Rocky's dwelling even gloomier.

As both star and writer, Stallone made changes as

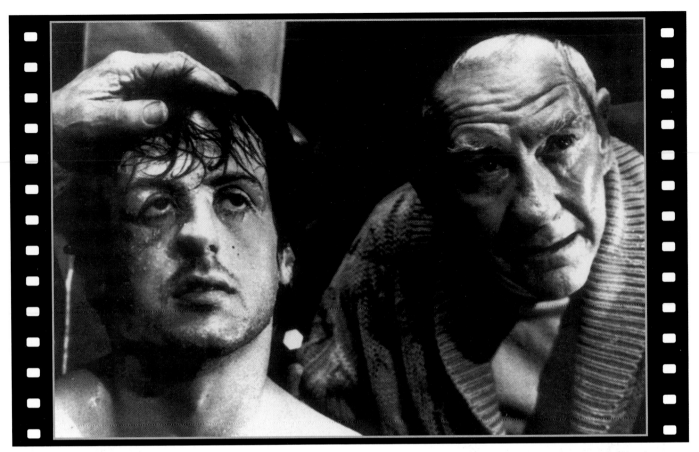

the need arose. Director John Avildsen felt Rocky's rejection of Mickey as his manager was followed too closely by Rocky's then trying to convince Mickey to change his mind. On the spot, Stallone improvised a powerful monologue after Mickey's departure, with Rocky shouting out his frustrations—"That's right, it stinks"—and pounding the bathroom door. It was a perfect touch, and Avildsen was astonished that Stallone nailed it in one take—only to have the soundman inform him the batteries in the recorder had died. So Stallone had to improvise it all over again. Fortunately, however, only one take was needed when he drank down the five raw eggs.

But the images from *Rocky* that remain most memorable are the training sequences and the climactic fight with Creed. The training scenes were shot at dawn on days as cold as they appeared in the film. There were no permits obtained and little planning—the fires really were burning outside the Italian market and someone just happened to toss Stallone an orange as he jogged by.

Each training sequence culminates with Rocky ascending the steps of the Art Museum, huffing and puffing slowly the first time, and sprinting two steps at a time and raising his arms in victory the second time. The two shots were actually filmed an hour apart, just before and just after sunrise. To demonstrate his strength on that triumphant second journey, he was originally supposed to carry Butkus, but hauling the 135-pound dog proved too much of a challenge.

Both Stallone and Weathers, a former football star, diligently trained and studied boxing before and during the filming of the movie. Avildsen realized early on that for the climactic fight scene to be believable, it would have to be worked out before filming in the ring. So he had Stallone choreograph an "exact ballet," breaking each round into sections and the ring into quarters, so each fighter knew exactly where to stand as the action unfolded. "For all the hours that we put in training," Stallone said, "it broke down to thirty-five hours of boxing rehearsal for each minute of fighting, whereas in most fight films you spend perhaps an hour or two rehearsing each round."

Again, the slim production budget prohibited the hiring of enough extras to fill the entire fight arena for the big bout between Rocky and Apollo. During the few overhead shots of the fight, empty seats are visible. To create the illusion of a packed arena, stock footage of fans at real fights was edited into the movie to show a big crowd.

At the last minute, Avildsen and Stallone persuaded the producers to spend money on large banners of Rocky and Creed to make the scene more imposing. When Rocky's likeness had on the wrong trunks, Avildsen made the most of the mistake, incorporating it into the script as another blow to Rocky's confidence. Similarly, Rocky's robe was made too large, and they couldn't afford a new one, so Stallone improvised lines to acknowledge the bagginess.

As for the finale, Stallone knew all along that Rocky would go the distance but lose the fight. In the second draft of his script, Stallone envisioned Rocky climbing out the ring and back into anonymity. Avildsen shot an ending with Apollo being carried out by a joyous crowd. Finally, Stallone devised the famous emotional ending. After barely surviving the fight, a bruised and bloodied Rocky stands in the ring as reporters badger him for his attention, while all Rocky wants is to find Adrian. "A-dri-an! . . . A-dri-an!" he yells, as she frantically pushes her way through the mob, between the ropes, and into his arms. As they profess their love for each other in a locked embrace, the scene freezes on the final heart-lifting image.

Rocky became an American folk hero and a motion picture phenomenon that racked up over $100 million at the box office. The tale of perseverance and redemption touched a nerve with America, prompting another champion of the underdog, famed director Frank Capra, to comment, "Boy, that's a picture I wish I had made."

BOXING MOMENTS

Violence, danger, corruption, and long-shot dreams—boxing has it all. Not surprisingly, Hollywood has returned again and again to fight films. Few of them transcend the genre or truly capture life inside the ring, but those that do are among the cinema's classics.

Body and Soul (1947) Charlie Davis (John Garfield) becomes a boxer to support his family, but success leads to temptation. He pursues the good life with a vengeance even though it means turning his back on loved ones and selling his soul to unethical promoters. In his final fight as champion, he suddenly decides after twelve rounds that he can't follow through and take a dive. He fights the last three rounds with a brutal fury that shakes up viewers and floors his opponent.

Somebody Up There Likes Me (1956) It's hard to believe that the director of *The Sound of Music* concocted two of the finest boxing flicks ever made, but Robert Wise's *The Set-Up* (1949) is an overlooked real-time classic about low-rent boxers near the end of the line. In *Somebody*, he made a star of Paul Newman as Rocky Graziano, the up-from-the-streets champ. The real Graziano tutored Newman and choreographed the final fight with Tony Zale (Court Shepard), which also features superb cinematography. Quick cuts between close-ups and long shots make this slugfest seem heart-pounding and true. This Rocky is the original.

The Harder They Fall (1956) Humphrey Bogart's underrated last film is about an aging sportswriter who takes a publicity job for a crooked boxing syndicate. The bosses fix the fights for their inept but appealing South American giant, while Bogie's Eddie Willis pumps up the media hype. The tanked fights are clumsy and ugly—exactly as they should be in this seedy world. The darkest moment comes when one fighter refuses at the last minute to get knocked out in front of his family and friends. The "compromise" is to put chicken wire in his mouth—when he gets hit blood will gush out and the fight will be stopped, but at least he'll still be standing. The only thing really compromised is everybody's morals.

Requiem for a Heavyweight (1962) Boxing inspires a frenzied bloodlust in crowds, but few see what life is like back in the dressing room for the ordinary boxer. In the heartbreaking scene that sets *Requiem* in motion, the doctor tells "Mountain" Rivera's cynical manager Maish Rennick (Jackie Gleason) that the punch-drunk Mountain (Anthony Quinn) can't fight any more because he might be blinded. When Rennick, who views his world with open eyes ("Sport? Are you kidding? If there was headroom they'd hold these things in sewers"), breaks the news to his washed-up fighter, Mountain is at a loss. "What do I do now? A guy's gotta do something." What he's forced to do will make fight fans stop and think next time they scream for blood.

Raging Bull (1980) Slow-motion camera work; blood, sweat, and spit flying everywhere; exaggerated sounds of violence; startling flashes from ringside cameras—it's hyper-stylized, but maybe that's the point. Jake La Motta's fight scenes as interpreted by Martin Scorsese and Robert De Niro capture the visceral energy of boxing better than any other drama.

Bonus Round

When We Were Kings (1996) Boxing films have featured plenty of acting heavyweights—from Newman to De Niro—but for pure charisma, Muhammad Ali remains the Greatest. This documentary of his historic 1974 bout with George Foreman in Zaire is compelling all the way through. But when Ali and Foreman finally face off, it is boxing unlike anything captured in a fictional drama. The rope-a-dope and fisticuffs here are the stuff of legend. Rumble, young man, rumble.

NATIONAL LAMPOON'S
ANIMAL HOUSE

1978

Fictitious Faber College, with its motto of mediocrity, "Knowledge is good," was the setting for *National Lampoon's Animal House,* the 1978 raucous parody of college fraternity life. The movie follows the antics of the oddballs of the Delta house as they battle a rival frat and an administration bent on expelling them under the threat of "double secret probation" while engaging in food fights, toga parties, and road trips, and dancing to "Shout." Despite the movie's paltry $3 million budget and largely unknown cast, audiences responded to the archetypal characters, making it the second biggest hit of the year behind *Grease,* and the highest-grossing comedy of its time.

All the debauchery and gross jokes came from the bright and literary minds of Doug Kenney, Chris Miller, and Harold Ramis, who showed that a coming-of-age movie could be rebellious and antiestablishment— could even wallow in immaturity and drunken revelry—without descending into mindlessness or losing its sense of humor.

The collaboration actually began with Ramis and Kenney. Kenny was a Harvard University graduate who had written for the venerated college humor magazine *Harvard Lampoon* and became editor-in-chief of the fledgling *National Lampoon* magazine. Their initial effort

was a movie script for an outlandish high school comedy called *Laser Orgy Girls*. *Lampoon* publisher Matty Simmons, who eventually coproduced *Animal House* with Ivan Reitman, told them that a film about underage high schoolers couldn't get away with the sex and drugs content of the script. So Ramis and Kenney switched the setting to college and recruited Chris Miller, who had been writing stories about his partying days at Dartmouth for *National Lampoon*. Miller claimed he had to "tone down" his experiences to make them believable.

The three writers sat for hours in a Greenwich Village bar irrigating their memories with Bloody Marys and writing down all the funny stories from their own college days. They ultimately produced a one-hundred-page outline, which they passed around to one another seven times before completing the script.

Animal House brings to life the rambunctious fra-ternal doings of the fictitious Delta house, particularly the womanizing Otter and his sidekick Boon, biker D-Day, the goofy freshman pledges Pinto and Flounder, and the spiritual heart of the group, Bluto Blutarsky, a character that director John Landis once described as "a cross between Harpo Marx and the Cookie Monster." The Deltas battle the stodgy Omegas and the venal Dean Wormer while partying, playing pranks, failing tests, and partying some more.

The first studio to see the script, Warner Bros., passed on the movie, and although Universal chief Ned Tanen loathed the concept, he was persuaded by some younger, hipper executives and by *National Lampoon*'s following to toss out a mere $3 million to make the movie. To direct their picture, the producers hired the relatively inexperienced John Landis, who had just completed the low-budget teen comedy *Kentucky Fried Movie*.

Landis, a Californian and a high school dropout, initially felt tension between him and the three writers, but there were ultimately few problems on the set—Miller and Kenney even took small parts in the film. As Hardbar, Miller voted to allow a freshman into the fraternity because "We need the dues," while Kenney's character Stork confronted the Delta's dismal fate with the utterance, "What the hell we spoz to do, ya moron?" Only Ramis sat out—he had written the part of Boon for himself but when he auditioned, Landis thought he looked too old and cast Peter Riegert instead.

The only actor who was seemingly irreplaceable was John Belushi, already a star on *Saturday Night Live*. The slovenly character of Bluto had been written with Belushi in mind, and at $40,000, the producers paid him far more than his costars. Belushi brought along his wife, Judith, who played his date at the toga party, dancing to "Shout" and later sitting on the stairs when Bluto demolished the folk singer's guitar. Belushi was so dynamic he began taking over every scene, so Landis adjusted the movie around Bluto. Although he played up Belushi's role, Landis cut the actor's lines to force him to rely on his marvelous facial expressions.

According to lore, Belushi's friend and fellow *SNL* player Dan Aykroyd was offered the role of D-Day but turned it down. Actor Bruce McGill got the part instead. The part of Otter went to Tim Matheson, who had originally been offered a role as one of the stodgy Omegas but requested to be one of the Deltas instead. By contrast, Mark Metcalf wanted to play Otter, but when Landis saw him, the director pegged him as the hateful militant Doug Neidermeyer.

Martha Smith auditioned for Mandy, but after realizing she'd have to strip for Belushi's peeping-Tom scene, she switched to Babs. When Stephen Furst walked in for his audition, the young actor nervously asked, "Am I supposed to read all the parts or just my part?" prompting Landis and everyone else in the room to simultaneously proclaim him "Flounder."

Final funding from the studio was contingent on Landis's casting at least one veteran star so he called in a personal favor. Donald Sutherland was a family friend, and Landis had even baby-sat for Sutherland's son Kiefer. Sutherland agreed to two days of shooting as

the pot-smoking, coed-seducing Professor Dave Jennings. To score the movie Landis tapped another family friend, acclaimed composer Elmer Bernstein.

Once again, the slim budget meant Landis couldn't afford much in the way of a set, so he decided to shoot on a real campus. After being rejected by fifty colleges, Landis received permission from the University of Oregon at Eugene to shoot on their campus for thirty days. However, the movie's climactic homecoming parade was shot in Cottage Grove, Oregon, about twenty miles south of Eugene. The Delta house's exterior scenes were shot at a local community center; when the building was torn down in 1986, the bricks sold as souvenirs for $5 each.

Landis brought all the actors who played Deltas up to Eugene early so they would have time to bond with one another. The Delta cast members became so close that when the actors portraying the rival Omegas

arrived in Eugene, including film novice Kevin Bacon, the Deltas attacked them in a real-life food fight. The Omega actors complained of feeling ostracized throughout the shoot.

Landis employed a collaborative approach by asking each actor to contribute a special "skill" to his character. McGill really could play "The William Tell Overture" by tapping his fingers against his throat; James Widdoes, who played Robert Hoover, juggled tennis rackets; and Belushi had a knack for crushing beer cans on his forehead.

Landis also encouraged improvisation, and several famous moments were born on the spot: Producer Matty Simmons contributed Bluto's line at the end when he moans, "Seven years of college down the

drain"; Smith ad-libbed the spelling out of "pig" as in "That boy is a P-I-G pig!" in Belushi's memorable zit impersonation scene; during the dancing to "Shout" at the toga party, Kenney suggested that Landis include the "Gator," where everyone falls to the floor and writhes uncontrollably. And when Boon catches his girlfriend Katy, played by Karen Allen, with Jennings, Allen refused to show any naked skin until Sutherland reportedly interjected, "I'll show my buns if you'll show yours." That compromise was captured in the scene.

Within the first year of its release, *National Lampoon's Animal House* raked in an astonishing $120 million, launched the National Lampoon movie franchise—which later included Chevy Chase's *Vacation* series—and boosted the young careers of virtually everyone involved from Tom Hulce (Pinto) to producer Ivan Reitman, with Belushi catapulting to moviestardom. *National Lampoon's Animal House* is listed among the American Film Institute's 100 Funniest American Movies of All Time, and nearly a quarter of century after its release, it was added to the Library of Congress's prestigious National Film Registry. For the ultimate coming-of-age movie with "a morally casual attitude," the party never ends.

For the writers, producers, and most of the cast, *Animal House* was their first major motion picture experience. Here's what they did with their education.

JOHN BELUSHI (Bluto)

Voted Most Likely to Complete a Mission from God: Joliet Jake in *The Blues Brothers*

TOM HULCE (Pinto)

Voted Best-Looking Guy in a Wig: Nominated for an Oscar as Wolfgang Mozart in *Amadeus*

TIM MATHESON (Otter)

Voted Most Charming Murderer: Alan Stanwyk in *Fletch*

PETER RIEGERT (Boon)

Voted Most Likely to Find Happiness in a Foreign Land: Mac MacIntyre in *Local Hero*

KAREN ALLEN (Katy)

Voted Best at Out-Drinking the Guys: Marion Ravenwood in *Raiders of the Lost Ark*

BRUCE MCGILL (D-Day)

Voted Most Likely to Undergo a Shocking Transformation: National Security Adviser Revell in *The Sum of All Fears*

KEVIN BACON (Chip)

Voted Best Dancer: Ren McCormack in *Footloose*

JOHN LANDIS (Director)

Voted Oddest Choice for Adviser to the King of Pop: Director of Michael Jackson's *Thriller*

HAROLD RAMIS (Writer)

Voted Most Likely to Succeed Again and Again: Writer-director for *Groundhog Day*, writer-director for *Analyze This*

IVAN REITMAN (Producer)

Voted Biggest Friend of Bill Murray: Directed *Meatballs*, *Stripes*, and *Ghostbusters*

ROBERT CRAY

Voted Most Likely to Make a Name for Himself: The uncredited bass player in Otis Day's Knights became the leading blues guitarist of the 1980s.

ALIEN

1979

If space science fiction films had been plagued for years by rather laughable space monsters, British director Ridley Scott's horror classic about a vicious chest-splattering, egg-laying carnivorous beast with a taste for human brains changed everything. *Alien* signaled an end to the days of bumbling actors wrapped in tinfoil and cheap rubber suits; it introduced audiences to a dark, disturbing vision that tapped something deep in the collective unconscious. Monster movies, and movie monsters, would never be the same.

Packed with sharp dialogue and gritty violence, *Alien* told the tale of a crew of space travelers forced to battle a devious, quickly evolving demon stowaway who murders them one by one, culminating in a final showdown with the film's heroine. While Dan O'Bannon's script was slammed by *Variety* for having "cardboard-cutout" characters and "more loose ends than the Pittsburgh Steelers," the public seemed willing to overlook its alleged shortcomings.

Bolstered by a massive advertising campaign with the chilling tag line "In space, no one can hear you scream," *Alien* was released on May 25, 1979, and quickly became a blockbuster, earning more than $60 million and finishing fourth for the year in box office receipts behind *Rocky II, Every Which Way but Loose,* and *Superman: The Movie.* In a year that witnessed double-digit inflation, a debilitating fuel crisis, and the hostages taken in Iran, the red-blooded heroics of Sylvester Stallone, Clint Eastwood, and Christopher Reeve undoubtedly offered relief from the pervading sense of powerlessness. But it was *Alien*'s lanky twenty-eight-year-old newcomer Sigourney Weaver who grabbed the national spotlight, landing on the cover of *Newsweek* as the harbinger of a new breed of female superstars.

Fueled by Weaver's performance as the tough-talking, flamethrower-wielding space rat Ripley, the film (which also starred Tom Skerritt, Ian Holm, John Hurt, Harry Dean Stanton, Yaphet Kotto, and Veronica Cartwright) presented a raw, gritty alternative to the year's more family-oriented sci-fi fare like *Star Trek: The Motion Picture* and *Buck Rogers in the 25th Century*. Scott's vision of the future had little in common with the orderly, antiseptic fantasies of traditional space tales. Unlike clean-living Captain James T. Kirk, the denizens of *Alien*'s cosmos enjoyed pornography, drank copious amounts of coffee, smoked cigarettes, cursed freely, and moaned about the paltriness of their paychecks, even while battling eight-foot extraterrestrials.

As refreshing as the idea of blue-collar astronauts might have been, what made *Alien* revolutionary was its look. Magnified by cinematographer Derek Vanlint's camera work and Jerry Goldsmith's haunting score, every detail, from the gloomy, claustrophobic interior of the spacecraft *Nostromo* to the windswept surface of the alien's planet, was skillfully designed to evoke an environment of anxiety and impending terror. And the key to that kingdom was the beast.

"I knew I was in dangerous waters regarding *Alien*'s creature from the start, because all of the 'monsters' I'd seen in other films were pretty tatty," Scott told biographer Paul M. Sammon. "Therefore, I had to find someone capable of taking our own beast up to the next level."

After Fox upped the picture's ante from $4.2 to $8.5 million on the strength of Scott's storyboards, the director turned to H. R. Giger, a Swiss surrealist famous for his elegantly grotesque paintings of half-organic,

ALIEN
HR Giger 78

half-machine creatures. Giger designed the alien in its various manifestations, including the egg; the hand-sized, acid-blooded "face hugger"; the fetal "chest burster"; and the hulking mature beast (whose gargantuan head, in a fitting stroke of macabre artistry, contained an actual human skull).

Despite the temptation to turn *Alien* into a gorier film, Scott generally minimized the violence. "I didn't want to go into overkill," he said. "I just wanted everything to be raw and real."

In one of the movie's more disturbing moments, Kane, played by John Hurt, regains consciousness after having his face attacked by a stingray-like creature while investigating an abandoned spaceship. The offending varmint, now dead, is locked away for future study by the *Nostromo*'s science officer, Ash (Holm). Relieved, the crew gathers for a celebratory dinner, oblivious to the fact that the creature has secreted a parasite into Kane's body. Seized by a coughing fit, which quickly turns into a full-blown seizure, Kane is held down on the table by the frightened crew. As blood sprays out of his chest, spattering the crew, he stops shuddering.

According to Scott, who wanted the authenticity of unrehearsed reactions, the only actor who knew what

would happen next was Hurt. "I didn't ever show [the actors] what would come out," Scott said. "They never saw that."

With Hurt's head poking through a hole in the table, Scott had a white T-shirted fiberglass torso screwed down to the tabletop and soaked with blood. When the moment came, special effects designer Roger Dicken rammed the chest burster from underneath the table through the torso in an explosion of blood and K-Y jelly.

As the horrified crew looks on, the tiny creature bares its razor-sharp teeth, squeals, and then shoots across the table on a specially built track, disappearing into the depths of the ship, where it quickly grows into the giant, steel-jawed killer of the film's later scenes.

In 2001, *TV Guide* named the chest burster scene one of the fifty greatest movie moments, and it was no doubt a pivotal factor in the Academy's decision to award *Alien* the 1979 Oscar for visual effects, although it lost to *All That Jazz* in the art direction category. Cable television's E! Network ranked *Alien* among the thirteen scariest movies of all time.

The film's success spawned a string of wildly popular sequels, all staring Weaver, by various directors:

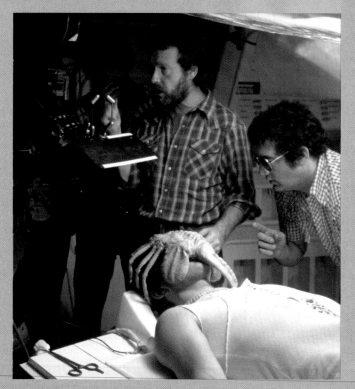

James Cameron's *Aliens* (1986), David Fincher's *Alien³* (1992), and Jean-Pierre Jeunet's *Alien: Resurrection* (1997). *Alien*, *Alien³*, and *Alien: Resurrection* are among the 250 highest grossing movies in history, and the entire corporate franchise has taken in more than $400 million in box office receipts to date. If the true measure of a film's success is the flattery of imitation, *Alien* is flush with rewards; its intense approach to futuristic production design, its use of a female action heroine, and its frightening imagery have influenced countless other movies, and it is widely considered a genre-defining classic.

For Scott, an accomplished director of television commercials, the film signaled his entry into Hollywood heavy-hitterdom and led to a string of acclaimed works, including *Blade Runner* (1982), *Thelma & Louise* (1991), *Gladiator* (2000), and *Black Hawk Down* (2001).

Interestingly enough, when Fox's U.K. director Sandy Lieberson approached him with the project in

1978, he had no interest in science fiction films, saying he considered them "silly."

Imagine what might not have been.

Unforgettable
SPACE SCI-FI

Ever since French magician and film pioneer Georges Méliès wowed audiences with his 1902 sensation *A Trip to the Moon,* filmgoers have willingly embarked on countless space adventures to distant galaxies to encounter a universe of alien life-forms. Here are some of the more unforgettable movie moments from the cosmos.

Forbidden Planet (1956) An unlikely success story, *Forbidden Planet* retold Shakespeare's *Tempest* in outer space. The movie starred Leslie Nielsen, Walter Pidgeon, and Anne Francis, and it influenced both *Star Trek* creator Gene Roddenberry and *Star Wars* creator George Lucas. But it is best remembered for introducing one of sci-fi's most beloved creations, Robby the Robot (voiced by Marvin Miller). His first appearance captivated viewers and led to roles in the film *The Invisible Boy* and guest appearances on TV's *Lost in Space.*

2001: A Space Odyssey (1968) Stanley Kubrick's quintessential sci-fi in space movie is filled with memorable moments. Two scenes in particular brilliantly married the visual and aural experiences of the film—the opening with Richard Strauss's "Thus Spake Zarathustra" (now thought of as the *2001* theme) and the scene in which the shuttle docks at the space station choreographed to the tune of Johann Strauss's waltz "Blue Danube."

Star Wars (1977) A long time ago, in a movie theater not so far away, George Lucas single-handedly revived the space sci-fi genre with this epic blockbuster. The movie meshed numerous classic ideals from ancient myths and American Westerns and created its own mythology. The pivotal moment in the first film comes when Old Ben, revealed as Jedi Obi-Wan Kenobi (Alec Guinness), begins teaching young Luke Skywalker (Mark Hamill) to be a Jedi knight—to wield a light saber and to control the force that we all soon hoped was with each of us.

Star Trek II: The Wrath of Khan (1982) After a disappointing feature-film debut, the *Enterprise* crew bounced back in this installment, one of the best films in the *Star Trek* series. At the movie's climax, the venomous Khan blows up his own spaceship in the hope of taking the *Enterprise* with it, but Spock—doing the "logical" thing—saves his comrades by sacrificing his life so the *Enterprise* can reach warp speed and escape. It's a finale with high tension, stellar effects, and one of sci-fi's more intimate moments as Kirk watches Spock die. And, of course, it also perfectly set up the next *Star Trek* sequel.

Total Recall (1990) Douglas Quaid (Arnold Schwarzenegger) must save Mars and its mutants from the evil Vilos Colhaagen (Ronny Cox). Quaid's finest moment comes when he appears to go down in a hail of bullets fired by Colhaagen's henchmen but then reveals himself to be a hologram—the real Quaid sneaks up and mows down the bad guys. The greatest effect is the ending when Colhaagen, Quaid, and love interest Melina (Rachel Ticotin) are hurled from the protective domes out into Mars's airless environment; the extreme lack of oxygen causes their faces, especially their eyes, to distort and bulge and then bulge some more, creating an image difficult to shake.

RAIDERS OF THE LOST ARK

1981

One of the most successful, beloved, and memorable movie serials is itself a tribute to the movies. The Indiana Jones trilogy pays homage to the Republic serials of the 1930s and 1940s. It was a vintage poster of a dashing hero jumping from a horse to a truck that stirred filmmaker George Lucas's childhood memories of Saturday afternoons at the movies watching serials like *Spy Smasher* and *Don Winslow of the Navy*. Those adventures were the spark that led to the creation of Dr. Henry "Indiana" Jones Jr., a character Lucas envisioned as "an archaeologist who was, on one hand, a treasure hunter, but one who had values that were tested."

Unlike the heroes of the serials, Jones was no clean-shaven, square-jawed matinee idol; he was a wisecracking adventurer with a three-day beard, a battered leather jacket, a well-worn felt fedora, and a deadly bullwhip. Not to mention a Ph.D.

Raiders of the Lost Ark was introduced to Steven Spielberg during a vacation with George Lucas in Hawaii in May 1977 on the same weekend *Star Wars* debuted.

The two longtime buddies sat together on the beach and discussed future projects. Spielberg had just completed *Close Encounters of the Third Kind,* and he mentioned that he would love to do a James Bond–type spy movie. Lucas told him he had a better

idea and laid out the whole Indiana Jones saga. Spielberg also loved serials, and six months later, after original director Philip Kaufman dropped out, Spielberg was given the job.

Actor Tom Selleck was the first choice for the film's archaeologist-adventurer. Selleck had already begun shooting his signature series, *Magnum P.I.,* and although the show hadn't yet aired, CBS refused to let him do the movie. So Spielberg went looking.

The young director searched for someone extraordinary—someone who could "become" Indiana Jones. He wanted a movie star, but not a "Dudley Do-Right with perfect teeth." George Lucas suggested Harrison Ford. After working with him on *American Graffiti* and the first two installments of *Star Wars,* Lucas was confident that Ford would be perfect for the role.

It took only a one-hour meeting between Ford and Spielberg three weeks before shooting was to begin for the director to agree. And where Ford's portrayal of

Han Solo in the initial episodes of the *Star Wars* saga made him a star, his turn as Indiana Jones catapulted him into the acting stratosphere, a position he has maintained ever since. In fact, Harrison Ford remains the highest-grossing movie star on the planet—his films have grossed over $5.5 billion worldwide.

Karen Allen was cast to play Indiana's love interest in the movie, Marion Ravenwood; Spielberg says he

chose her because she was "spunky with a real twinkle in her eye—and someone who was tough and direct." The director felt she was a great match for Ford. "I wanted to see what would happen when I put these two demons together," he said.

One of the movie's signature scenes concludes the fantastic opening sequence in the booby-trapped Temple of the Chachapoyan Warriors, which was set in the jungles of South America but actually built on a sound-stage at Elstree Studios just outside of London. Jones survives all the deadly pitfalls laid out before him and grabs the golden idol. Unfortunately, that act unleashes a giant boulder that pursues him all the way out of the cave. Because the movie was shot in the early days of computer animation, the boulder actually existed. Since Harrison Ford had deemed it his acting mission to make his peril completely believable, he actually had to outrun the boulder.

Of course, the sphere chasing Indy wasn't made by Mother Nature—it was a twelve-foot prop constructed of plaster, wood, and fiberglass—but it still weighed over three hundred pounds. When the time came for filming, the scene was shot twice from five different angles, meaning Ford had to outrun the boulder ten times. Spielberg later admitted, "He won ten times and beat the odds. He was lucky, and I was an idiot for letting him try."

Actually, the stunt that followed Indiana's escape from the temple was much more dangerous. After outrunning the blowgun-wielding natives, Indy jumps into a river, swims to a seaplane, and just barely escapes more deadly darts. As the plane lifts off, Indy clings to the cockpit door, which remains open. The problem was that the door had to be closed for the pilot to control the plane's rudder. Just as the aircraft flew out of camera range, it crashed into a stand of mangrove trees. Luckily, the seaplane was only fifteen or twenty feet off the ground when the pilot lost control.

Though the plane was damaged, the pilot and Ford emerged virtually unscathed.

Another memorable scene in *Raiders* takes place in the Well of Souls, a huge buried temple set also on a soundstage at Elstree. The producers had ordered two thousand snakes to fill the floor, but when they tested the set and spread out the snakes, the reptiles barely covered a quarter of the space. So they brought in another three thousand mechanical snakes made of rubber and operated by wires. When operators manipu-

lated the wires controlling the phony snakes, however, each group wriggled in unison. Spielberg says it made them look like "the June Taylor Dancers." So the rubber snakes got their slithering papers, and Spielberg asked his crew to find him more real snakes.

Production assistants were sent to every pet shop in London, and when it came time to drop Ford and Allen into the writhing set, there were close to seven thousand live snakes underfoot. Unlike his snake-hating character, Ford was not afraid of the reptiles. In fact, as a boy he had collected snakes, so his fright was strictly for the camera. But the creatures really frightened Karen Allen, who was doubled whenever it was possible (sometimes by a male animal wrangler who shaved his legs and put on Karen's dress).

It wasn't snakes but a bug that got to Harrison Ford on location in Tunisia—a microscopic bug that motivated the scene that earns the movie's biggest laugh. It's a showdown between Indy and a turbaned Arab swordsman armed with a giant crescent blade. Instead of battling the behemoth with bullwhip and fists, Jones unexpectedly dispatches him with a single shot from his sidearm.

That denouement wasn't scripted; according to Ford it was a device he thought up to get him back to his hotel quickly. The actor explained, "I was into my fifth week of dysentery, and I was riding in at 5:30 A.M. with nothing to do but submit to wild imaginings. So I stormed Steven with the idea of just dismissing this maniac. I said, 'Let's just shoot him.' And we did."

With its innovative action sequences, nail-biting stunts, and never-before-seen technical feats created by Lucas's own special effects company, Industrial Light & Magic, *Raiders of the Lost Ark* was a

breathlessly paced $23 million thrill ride. Appreciative audiences packed theaters throughout the summer of 1981, and the film racked up more than $300 million at the box office worldwide, increasing Hollywood's appetite for big-budget blockbusters. *Raiders of the Lost Ark* received eight Academy Award nominations and won four. It spawned two sequels: *Indiana Jones and the Temple of Doom* in 1984, which prompted the movie ratings board to create the PG-13 rating; and *Indiana Jones and the Last Crusade* in 1989.

What began as a high-budget tribute to the old Saturday matinee serials developed into a genuine film phenomenon. The treasure-hunting adventures of Lucas and Spielberg's whip-wielding hero proved to be a timeless tale that has rightfully found its place among the classics of motion picture history.

Unforgettable
HARRISON FORD MOMENTS

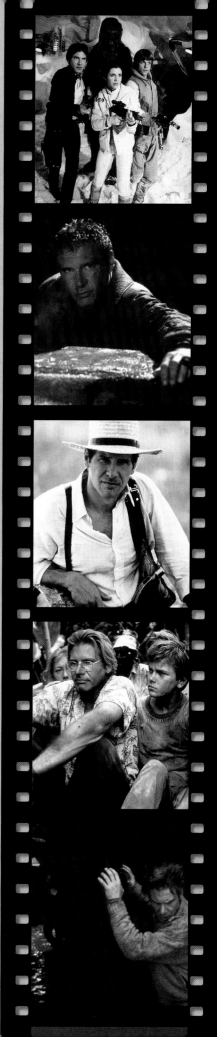

Harrison Ford will forever be linked with two of the most popular franchises in movie history—as Indiana Jones in *Raiders* and as Han Solo in *Star Wars*. He has spent his career doing star turns in action flicks, but Ford has never stopped creating memorable, very human heroes.

The Empire Strikes Back (1980) Ford had plenty of great scenes in *Star Wars* (1977) as freelance pilot Han Solo: snarling at Princess Leia (Carrie Fisher), "Look your worshipfulness, I take orders from just one person—me," and risking his life to save the rebels. But his charismatic machismo is at its finest in *Empire* when Solo heads into the deep freeze and Princess Leia tearfully confesses, "I love you." Without batting an eye, he confidently smirks, "I know." That's keeping your cool.

Blade Runner (1982) When film noir meets sci-fi, Ford manages to pull off a futuristic Bogie. His Rick Deckard character starts off unwilling to stick his neck out but gradually realizes that he must take a stand. The turning point comes when Rachael (Sean Young) arrives at his apartment after he has identified her as a replicant. He starts off with a sneer, shutting the door in her face, and proceeds to drill her with the truth. Then her emotional response moves him to empathy and a reexamination of his own beliefs and behaviors. The dialogue is terse, and the room is dark, but Ford conveys the churning depths of his character throughout.

Witness (1985) Ford's Oscar-nominated role as John Book, a Philadelphia detective who must associate with the Amish to investigate police corruption, has plenty of the requisite tough-guy hero moments. But Ford shines brightest in his scenes with his Amish love interest, Rachel, played by Kelly McGillis, especially in the barn when she helps Book fix his car. The radio comes on playing Sam Cooke's "Wonderful World," and Book crosses the line. He begins dancing with Rachel—intensely, flirtatiously, playfully—and we see not only Ford's charisma but also a joyful side he rarely shows.

Mosquito Coast (1986) The passionate, manic, unlikable inventor Allie Fox—a role originally intended for Jack Nicholson—is Ford's most emotionally complex character and reportedly his favorite. Fox creates a new world for his family in the middle of the jungle, where he builds an entire village and a tremendous machine that can provide ice and refrigeration without electricity. When Fox's hubris unwittingly attracts gun-toting criminals, he traps them in the machine to kill them, but they inadvertently blow it up and ignite an entire village. Ford transforms himself again and again, from the arrogant man moralizing to his son Charlie (River Phoenix) about why it's okay to kill, to the horrified "father" watching his beloved baby (his invention) die, to the never-say-die optimist who rationalizes away failure rather than learn from it. Through it all, Fox remains a memorable character with fire in his eyes.

The Fugitive (1993) Ford stars as Doctor Richard Kimble, a man on the run from the law after being falsely accused of murdering his wife. The action scenes—especially when Kimble escapes a prison bus just as a train crashes into it and flees from U.S. Marshal Samuel Gerard (Tommy Lee Jones) by leaping from a dam into a waterfall—are the heart-stopping highlights. Ford makes his mark at the end when he simultaneously battles villain Charles Nichols (Jeroen Krabbe) and tries to stay one step ahead of his police pursuer, Lt. Gerard. In a lesser actor's hands, this sequence might seem far-fetched, but Ford's solid grounding invests emotional reality into this thrilling finale.

E.T.: THE EXTRA-TERRESTRIAL

1982

It was 1982. Former movie star Ronald Reagan's presidency was in its second year. Federal authorities were hunting a lunatic lacing Tylenol bottles with cyanide. Aussie band Men At Work dominated the airwaves. And the world was enraptured by a visit from an extra-terrestrial.

Unlike the terrifying alien invasion depicted in the 1938 radio drama *War of the Worlds,* which left panicked listeners drawing their shades and running for cover, this creature from outer space, an endearing figment of director Steven Spielberg's imagination, left moviegoers looking longingly into the sky and yearning for a real-life encounter with the being they had come to know as E.T.

The idea for *E.T.* materialized one day while Spiel-berg was directing the adventure film *Raiders of the Lost Ark* on location in the middle of the Tunisian desert. He was pondering the seashells he had come across in the sand. Thousands of miles away from his home in Los Angeles, he recalled feeling alone and "a bit separated" from himself. In that moment, he found inspiration. Over the next few days, a story evolved in Spiel-berg's mind about a lonely boy who finds the most unlikely friend right in his own backyard.

Serendipitously, screenwriter Melissa Mathison was also on the *Raiders* set, visiting her soon-to-be-husband Harrison Ford. Mathison had penned the script for the 1979 movie *The Black Stallion,* based on the poignant novel about a young boy stranded on a deserted island

with a wild horse. Spielberg asked Mathison to write the screenplay for a new film. At the time, neither of them could know that it was the beginning of the cinematic legend *E.T.: The Extra-Terrestrial*.

Spielberg had long been fascinated with the idea of space travel and aliens from other worlds. His father was a sci-fi buff, constantly reading books about terrifying creatures from outer space that sought dominion over Earth. Spielberg's dad also instilled in him the perception that technologically advanced space travelers would probably be more benevolent, and that was the idea behind Spielberg and Mathison's friendly three-foot-tall E.T.

It took Mathison only eight weeks to finish the first draft, which Spielberg read in about an hour. The story

about a boy who befriends and shelters an abandoned alien was rich in meaning and subtext, with relevance for any child suffering from loneliness. Profoundly moved by the script, Spielberg admitted that his empathy for E.T.'s predicament was partly born out of his own forlorn feelings about his parents' divorce.

Excitedly, he took the project to Sidney Sheinberg, then head of Universal Pictures, who green-lighted *E.T.* almost immediately.

Dee Wallace was cast as Mary, the mother of three kids who was struggling emotionally over her recent separation from her husband. Fourteen-year-old Robert McNaughton landed the part of eldest son Michael. Spielberg was impressed by his experience as a young

stage actor and his remarkable professionalism. Drew Barrymore, the six-year-old daughter of actor John Drew Barrymore and great-niece of Lionel Barrymore, was picked for the role of Gertie, the adorable, precocious little sister.

Spielberg had first met Barrymore while casting *Poltergeist*. Although Barrymore didn't get a part in that movie, Spielberg was so impressed by her rambunctious spirit and her proclivity to make up stories that he encouraged her to come back for future projects. He had already auditioned many kids for the part of Gertie, but when Barrymore came in, she brashly announced that she could improve his movie, and he cast her on the spot.

Finding the right actor to play E.T.'s human soul mate, Elliot, was an ordeal. Spielberg had already auditioned more than one hundred kids when a colleague steered him toward a bright nine-year-old actor from San Antonio, Texas, named Henry Thomas. The audition was a heart-wrenching experience for everyone in the room. Borrowing a scenario from the film, Spielberg told Thomas to imagine that he had an alien in his house, that the creature was his friend, and that a man from NASA was going to try to take it away. The audition was videotaped with casting director Mike Fenton assuming the role of the NASA official.

"No! You can't take him away; he's mine," asserted Thomas, his eyes welling up with tears.

"But it's not my choice—the president asked me to come here and get him," Fenton replied.

Thomas cried defiantly, "I don't care what the president says—he's my best friend, and you can't take him away!"

"Okay, kid," interrupted Spielberg, "you got the job."

Thomas's emotional intuition and irreverent response could not have been more accurate. Defying authority was one of the core themes in the story.

The movie opens with E.T. foraging through the woods under cover of night, lifting a sapling from the soft floor of the redwood forest. It's revealed that he is right on the outskirts of the city. Suddenly, trucks come roaring up, and several men carrying flashlights leap out and start chasing the little creature through the forest. The men's faces are cast in shadow to imply the impersonal face of adult authority. The concept of childhood innocence at odds with an indifferent adult world permeates the film.

Panicked, E.T. scurries desperately through the woods, trying to escape his pursuers. Actually, it was only a mounted red light moving along a track behind a thicket of ferns, but the illusion was effective. E.T. cries as he tries to make it to his spaceship, but he's too late and is abandoned. The infantlike cry that evoked sympathy for the little stranded alien was actually the recorded squeal of a sea otter.

Indeed, in stark contrast to the menacing space creatures from the sci-fi films of the 1950s, there was nothing remotely frightening about E.T. With big sad eyes, he looked a bit like a tortoise without its shell. E.T.'s creator, Carlo Rambaldi, actually modeled E.T.'s eyes on the knowing, saddened look that Spielberg saw in the eyes of Albert Einstein, Ernest Hemingway, and Carl Sandburg.

Given the limitations of special effects technology in the early '80s, it was indeed a tall order to create the realistic little creature. But Rambaldi, who had worked on *Close Encounters of the Third Kind,* and his crew of special effects artists were up to the task. In all, three different models were devised: a mechanical E.T. attached to control boxes that were manipulated by twelve different operators, a radio-controlled electronic version for facial close-ups, and an E.T. suit, worn by special E.T. movement performers. The latter was used for the scenes in which E.T. actually moved around the set. Rambaldi and team also constructed four interchangeable heads for E.T., each of which was equipped with a neck that could be raised and lowered like a miniature periscope.

The movie takes an emotional turn when Mary finally discovers E.T. in her home. It is clear that he is dying, yet her immediate maternal instinct is to protect her children from him. But when government scientists and doctors invade their home, her maternal instincts extend to her children's new best friend. The men from the government are all clad in helmeted white protective coverall suits, obscuring their identities in yet another statement about the cold, insensitive nature of

authority. But there's one exception: the sympathetic character of Keys, played by Peter Coyote, who tells Elliot that the presence of E.T. on Earth is "a miracle."

When the scene called for reviving the dying extra-terrestrial, Spielberg decided to use real doctors from the University of Southern California Medical Center instead of actors. He didn't think actors could assimilate all the medical jargon and play the scene convincingly.

Once E.T. is revived, Michael and Elliot kidnap the creature from the scientists to help him escape back to his home planet. As they ride their bikes at full speed toward a police roadblock, a suspense-filled confrontation is averted as E.T. summons his powers and the bikes take flight up into the sky. Audiences cheered, but Steven Spielberg winced. It had always bothered him that the police held rifles and pistols in the movie and that the children were menaced by that kind of threat from the authorities.

For the twentieth anniversary of E.T., Spielberg rereleased the film and employed state-of-the-art computer-generated visual effects to alter the scene. In the revised version, as the kids soar above the roadblock, the cops are no longer wielding guns and rifles but instead hold walkie-talkies in their hands.

If the tone during the film shoot was sometimes heartrending and somber, behind the scenes the making of E.T. was quite another matter. Spielberg created a family atmosphere on the set, getting to know all the players on a personal level to understand how they worked best. He played video games with Henry Thomas and treated Drew Barrymore like she was his own daughter. He even showed up to direct the Halloween scene in costume, dressed as a matronly schoolteacher. In retrospect, Spielberg muses that the cast of E.T. was like his first family. Drew Barrymore once said of the experience of making E.T., "I think in a lot of ways we were taught love."

In E.T., Spielberg created such an endearing character that the cast, crew, and millions of moviegoers were able to ignore the special effects and suspend disbelief. E.T. opened on June 11, 1982, to record box office and went on to gross over three quarters of a billion dollars worldwide. Spielberg asserts that while Schindler's List is his most significant film, E.T. remains his most personal. The movie's time-honored tale of innocence versus authority is universal, and that is the reason it remains one of the most memorable films in the history of modern cinema.

STEVEN SPIELBERG MOMENTS

No one in movie history is responsible for more Hollywood blockbusters and more unforgettable movie moments than Steven Spielberg, from *Jaws* to *Raiders of the Lost Ark* to *E.T.* to *Jurassic Park*. But as the following list shows, Spielberg is capable of far more than just light-hearted action and special effects wizardry.

Close Encounters of the Third Kind (1977) The spaceship scene at the end is certainly a memorable spectacle, but the most Spielbergian scene comes early on when the aliens flying overhead bring a young boy's toys to life. Although his mother is terrified when she sees it, the boy is surprised, then mesmerized. This scene of suburbia gone askew simultaneously foreshadows both the fear of *Poltergeist* and the innocent wonder of *E.T.*

The Color Purple (1985) Spielberg's most underrated asset is his penchant for perfect casting and his most underrated accomplishment is this movie, which brought stardom to Whoopi Goldberg (Celie) and Oprah Winfrey (Sofia). When Sofia's husband, Harpo, asks Celie how to handle Sofia's feisty behavior, Celie responds simply, "Beat her," revealing how difficult it is to break centuries of learned behavior. Later, Sofia's enraged response shows hope for the future of these women.

Schindler's List (1993) This Holocaust saga is Spielberg's most mature and most sophisticated film, and it is one of the most powerful movies ever made. Astonishingly, the director's most memorable moment came from the smallest of details—the somber black-and-white tone is broken only by one small girl's red coat. We see her twice—walking in the concentration camp and then in a pile of corpses. Heartbreaking.

Saving Private Ryan (1998) No movie—not even a documentary—could ever truly capture the hell of war, especially the battle for the beaches on D-Day. No other moviemaker has come as close as Spielberg does in this dizzying, terrifying, and heart-stopping scene. There are no false steps or gratuitous shots in the entire sequence.

Minority Report (2002) After several years away from the flashy blockbusters he built his name on, Spielberg grabbed audiences with this movie's stunning opener. The first few moments offer confusing but compelling glimpses of a violent murder and spooky beings while jumping in time and shifting speeds. Then the scene plays out in real time as we learn about "precogs" and stopping "future murders" while Tom Cruise races with the clock to prevent what we have just witnessed from actually happening. The movie is only getting started, but the audience feels like catching its breath, if it can.

WALL STREET

1987

"How can a person still have any hopes who is addicted to the superficial,
who grubs with greedy hands for treasures . . ."
—FROM *FAUST,* BY GOETHE

Perhaps no era in modern history is better defined by excess and corporate greed than the 1980s. The stock market was booming. Hostile corporate takeovers, high-risk investment schemes, and insider trading scandals monopolized the news. It was the drama of this take-no-prisoners, cutthroat world of high finance, with its scheming and profiteering, that inspired director Oliver Stone to make a film that would capitalize on the mercurial swings of the market and the wavering morality of its high-powered investors. The decade of greed had arrived, and *Wall Street* was the perfect vehicle for Stone to tell a modern-day story of innocent ambition corrupted by malicious greed.

Having just won an Academy Award for his 1986 film *Platoon,* Stone was taking a big risk. Films about business had never been a sure thing at the box office, and like an investor trading commodities on the stock exchange, he knew *Wall Street* would be a long shot. But he also possessed an insider's savvy. His father, Lou Stone, had been a trader on Wall Street for most of his life. That personal background was Stone's original impetus to make a film that would pay homage to his father.

Wall Street's history is a testament to the resilience needed to make it in the movie business. Stone wrote the original screenplay at the age of thirty, sold the script when he was thirty-three, and finally got the opportunity to make the picture at forty-four. He enlisted the help of screenwriter Stanley Weiser, and a cleverly constructed plot emerged, replete with snappy one-liners and poignant speeches. They developed realistic, sympathetic characters giving the film believability and relevance to its era.

Also fresh from *Platoon* was its star, actor Charlie Sheen. In the opening scene, we are introduced to Sheen's character, Bud Fox, a junior account executive at a New York investment firm. Eager and determined to "get rich quick," Fox ignores the advice of the firm's senior manager, Lou Mannheim, a no-nonsense man of few words brilliantly portrayed by Hal Holbrook. Modeled after Stone's father, Mannheim is the voice of altruistic wisdom. "The thing about money," he tells Bud, "is that it makes you do things you don't wanna do."

The father-son theme permeates the movie. Early in the film, Fox gets burned on a bad investment and goes to borrow money from his father, Carl Fox, an airline mechanic played by Charlie Sheen's real-life father, veteran actor Martin Sheen. Stone had debated on whether to cast Sheen or Jack Lemmon for the part, but settled on Sheen at Charlie's behest.

"You made fifty grand last year," Carl Fox scolds. "Where the hell does it all go?"

"One day you're gonna be proud of me," Bud tells him.

"It's yourself you have to be proud of," the elder Fox replies.

Oliver Stone says this first exchange between a moralistic father and an idealistic son was drawn from his years as a struggling young writer, when he reluctantly borrowed money from his own dad.

Undaunted by setbacks, Bud sets his sites on "bagging the big elephant," billionaire Gordon Gekko, played by actor Michael Douglas. It was an unlikely role for the smooth and charming Douglas, who was best known as the costar of television's *The Streets of San Francisco*. Gekko comes across as arrogant and self-assured, but Douglas openly admits he was actually intimidated during the filming. He simply wasn't accustomed to playing "the bad guy," and he struggled with the extensive dialogue.

Stone had originally approached Richard Gere to play the ruthless Gekko, but the script was still unpolished, and Gere declined. Stone then courted Warren Beatty, but the studio backing the film, 20th Century Fox, liked Douglas, fresh from his success as Jack Colton in the 1984 romantic comedy *Romancing the Stone*.

Oliver Stone was hesitant, because Douglas lacked experience as a serious film actor. Once the two men met, however, Stone sensed that Douglas possessed the "genetic toughness" of his father, legendary actor Kirk Douglas. Stone saw "repressed anger" in Douglas and he tapped into it. At one point, a frustrated Stone came to Douglas's trailer and asked him if he was feeling okay. When Douglas responded that he felt fine, Stone retorted, "You look like you've never acted before." At the time, Douglas felt insulted, but he was able to transfer that emotion into his performance.

Despite Fox's awe of Gekko's fame and fortune, he is determined to get the high roller to invest, and he manages to pry his way into Gekko's office with a gift box of Cuban cigars. Entering the high-energy, high-tech office of the corporate trader, we meet the cold and calculating Gekko.

"So why am I listening to you?" Gekko demands of

a nervous Fox. Bud pitches some hot stocks, but Gekko dismisses each prospect with scorn. Fearing he has blown his one and only shot, Fox blurts out his father's company, Blue Star Airlines. To sell Gekko, he divulges confidential information about an imminent court settlement, which will exonerate the beleaguered carrier. In that moment, Fox realizes he has betrayed his father, but when Gekko calls him later that afternoon to buy twenty thousand shares, it's a dream come true.

The investment pans out, and Gekko rewards Fox by opening a million-dollar investment account with him, but he fires him just as quickly when the next investment tanks. It's a critical moment in the film. "I'm not just another broker," Fox pleads. "If you give me another chance, I'll prove that to you."

Gekko offers Fox a second chance if he'll help undermine an old rival, corporate raider Larry Wildman, played by British film star Terence Stamp. He tells a reluctant Fox to secretly follow Wildman.

"I could go to jail," Bud protests.

"That's inside information, isn't it?" Gekko tells Fox. "If you're not inside, you are outside."

It was one of the first scenes shot using what Michael Douglas recalls as "gorilla-style" camera work, right in their faces. Again, it was a difficult scene for Douglas, who had virtually all the dialogue.

In this sink-or-swim moment, Fox gives in. "Okay, Mr. Gekko, you got me." It's the beginning of Bud's ethical slide into the underbelly of high finance.

Fox tails Wildman and learns that he intends to buy a steel corporation. In a poison-pill plot, Gekko buys a large share of the company's stock, forcing

Wildman to buy him out at an inflated price. Gekko rewards Fox again with big money and big perks, one of which is the beautiful Darien Taylor, played by a luminous Daryl Hannah. Stone says her character symbolized the high-class spoiled and manipulative sycophants of the era, and Bud falls for her.

The film unfolds like a Faustian tale. Gekko acquires the controlling share of Blue Star Airlines and, making Bud the point man on the deal, plans to restructure the company. In a critical scene, all the union representatives agree to go along with the plan except for Carl Fox, who sees that Gekko really intends to cannibalize the airline and sell it off.

Bud follows his father out into the elevator for a showdown. He accuses his dad of undermining his success. The camera pans back and forth as Carl discounts

his son's superficial and pompous attitude. "What you see," he tells Bud, "is a guy who never measured a man's success by the size of his *wallet!*"

Martin Sheen delivered the last word with so much force that it took the younger Sheen by surprise. "It blew me out of my socks," Charlie would later reflect, because they hadn't rehearsed the scene that way. But the elder Sheen had decided he wanted to pay homage to George C. Scott's performance at the end of *The Hustler*, when he yelled at Paul Newman, "You owe me *money!*" Charlie came right back at his dad with equal force, also improvised, making the scene all the more believable.

Throughout production, Stone strived to make every element—from the seemingly incidental things people said down to the background set dressings—as

realistic and representative of Wall Street's fast-paced culture as possible. He even shot the trading scenes on the floor of the New York Stock Exchange, using real traders.

The moment that best captures the avaricious mood characteristic of the '80s comes when Gekko addresses a convention filled with stockholders of Teldar Paper, of which he is the majority shareholder. Teldar's management has warned everybody that Gekko will wreck the company. "I am not a destroyer of companies," Gekko says in his own defense. "I am a liberator of them. The point is, ladies and gentleman, that greed, for lack of a better word, is good. Greed is right. Greed works."

The "Greed is good" line was inspired by a quote from infamous Wall Street trader Ivan Boesky. At a commencement speech to a business school—before he was convicted of insider trading violations—Boesky offered, "Greed is all right. . . . I think greed is

healthy." The rest of Gekko's speech, proclaiming that greed would also save "that other malfunctioning corporation, the U.S.A.," was completely original.

Considering his anguish over the lengthy dialogues in the film, this three-page diatribe was a potential meltdown for Douglas, but by the time the scene was shot, Stone had pushed him to know his lines inside out. Douglas likened Stone's directorial style to an army commander who demanded dedication and loyalty from his soldiers. Having fully assimilated Gekko's merciless persona, he nailed the scene in the first few takes. It was the most celebrated moment in the film and in Michael Douglas's career.

The film's final turning point occurs when Bud realizes that his father was right; Gekko is out to wreck Blue Star for sheer profit. Bud turns the tables on Gekko. He makes a backroom deal with Gekko's old nemesis Larry Wildman to sabotage Gekko's plans to

sell off Blue Star. In return, Wildman agrees to restructure the company. It works, but Bud is arrested the next day for insider trading.

Cutting a deal with federal investigators, he meets Gekko in Central Park, wearing a hidden microphone. Fortuitously, it rained that day and was still drizzling when the scene was shot, providing a gloomy and dramatic light. Furious at being undermined by his protégé, Gekko sucker punches Bud, knocking him down and bloodying his lip. He then tosses him his handkerchief. The moment is particularly realistic on film because Douglas accidentally smacked Sheen during one of the takes.

Although he still goes to jail, Bud Fox rediscovers his moral character and redeems himself in the eyes of his father. And like Fox, audiences walked away from *Wall Street* pondering Oliver Stone's convincing message that greed is not good after all.

Ironically, executives at 20th Century Fox under-valued Stone's morality play and sold the film short. Instead, they heavily invested their promotional monies on *Broadcast News,* which came out the same year. A funny and timely film, *Broadcast News* was nominated for seven Academy Awards but garnered none of those dividends. *Wall Street* was nominated for just one category—Best Actor. Beating all expectations, Michael Douglas deservedly won the Oscar for his performance.

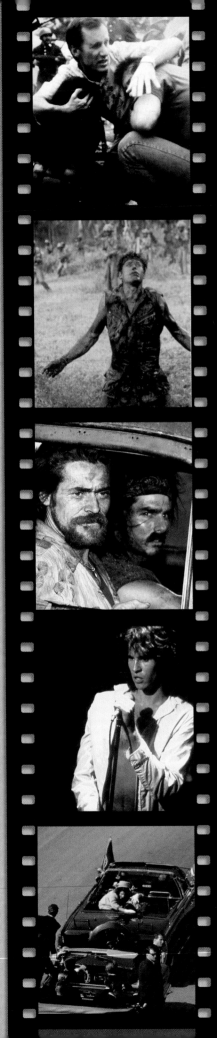

OLIVER STONE MOMENTS

From *Nixon* to *Natural Born Killers*, director Oliver Stone's movies have made a mark in Hollywood with their powerful characters and controversial subjects. Here are some of Stone's best and most influential films.

Salvador (1986) With this film about American hypocrisy during El Salvador's civil war, Stone established himself as a force to be reckoned with, a visceral filmmaker with a definite agenda who hits audiences over their heads to make his point and leaves them shaken. He announced that presence most powerfully in a scene in which war photographers Richard Boyle (James Woods) and John Cassady (John Savage) find themselves shooting at a body dump with moldering corpses mindlessly strewn about the landscape. The stench sickens Boyle and somehow seems palpable even to viewers.

Platoon (1986) The opening of *Saving Private Ryan* showed the terrifying hell that is war in a big-picture way. But *Platoon* showed what war does to the people who fight it in an intimate way. In a small Vietnamese village, Private Chris Taylor (Charlie Sheen) grows frustrated and sprays bullets at the feet of a maimed young boy; the boy remains stoic and Taylor is reduced to tears. Then the deranged Bunny (Kevin Dillon) murders the boy, and soon after, Staff Sergeant Bob Barnes (Tom Berenger) kills an innocent woman while Taylor watches helplessly. In fact, only the intervention of Sergeant Elias Grodin (Willem Dafoe) prevents Barnes from executing a young girl. The scene ends with the American troops torching the village. Taylor is finally roused to action when he angers his fellow soldiers by stopping them from raping young girls.

Born on the Fourth of July (1989) Stone is not a subtle director. He struggles as much with scoring political points as he does with generating genuine emotion. But in this, his most humane movie about a real-life war vet, he manages to pull it all together. Ron Kovic (Tom Cruise) comes home from Vietnam paralyzed and a hero to a country increasingly disillusioned with the war; Kovic gradually turns himself inside out and becomes a leader of the antiwar movement. The turning point comes with a visual masterpiece—in a July 4th parade that captures the nation's turmoil, Kovic is cheered by some and cursed by others.

The Doors (1991) When Jim Morrison (Val Kilmer) unravels completely, playing into the hands of his enemies by exposing himself during a drunken tirade at a Miami concert, Stone brilliantly captures the dangers of self-indulgence and believing your own legend.

JFK (1991) Stone's take on the Kennedy assassination theories comes to a head with attorney Jim Garrison's (Kevin Costner) closing argument in his attempt to prove a massive conspiracy. From Garrison's low-key debunking of the magic-bullet theory to the dissection of the Zapruder film merging real (and endlessly heartbreaking) footage, miniature models, and recreations, Stone presents the information in an utterly spellbinding attack. Is it all true? Not likely. Is it manipulative? Sure. But the scene is unforgettable, searing Stone's skepticism of the government's agenda into audiences' minds.

WHEN HARRY MET SALLY

1989

"It's just that all men are sure it's never happened to them, and most women, at one time or another, have done it. So you do the math."

—SALLY

In 1988, director Rob Reiner and producer Andrew Scheinman sat down with screenwriter Nora Ephron to discuss a potential project. Recently single after nearly ten years of marriage, the dejected forty-one-year-old Reiner was considering making a highly personal film about men, women, dating, and sex that he hoped would allow him to rectify the "complete and utter mess" he had made of his social life. Little did he know, the resulting picture would become one of Hollywood's all-time great romantic comedies.

When Harry Met Sally, which grew out of the trio's candid conversations, took audiences to the front lines of the gender wars, plumbing the depths of contentious male-female relationships and ripping the lid off a number of closely guarded sexual secrets. With quick-witted humor and a healthy dose of sentimentality, the movie offered a poignant look at the love-hate tango between two intelligent and highly neurotic New Yorkers: death-obsessed pessimist Harry Burns, played by Billy Crystal, and Pollyanna control freak Sally Albright, played by Meg Ryan. Over a twelve-year period, the two meet, feud, become friends, have sex, and eventually fall in love.

Opening on July 12, 1989, and taking in almost $9 million in its first weekend of wide release, *When Harry Met Sally* quickly became a sensation. Its subject matter ate up dozens of column inches in popular magazines and filled hours of TV talk-show programming. Can men and women be friends without the issue of sex getting in the way? Do single men really want to split instead of cuddle after making love? Are women truly prone to, well, pretending a little during sex? The public was suddenly obsessed.

In the press, the film drew frequent comparisons—both charitable and captious—to the work of director Woody Allen, the king of dysfunctional New York romance, and particularly to his Academy Award–winning 1977 film *Annie Hall*. One New York paper tagged *When Harry Met Sally* a "Woody Allen wanna-be, full of canned romance," and another "a Woody Allen movie . . . without the complexity of character."

Reiner admitted that it sometimes seemed as if he was following in Allen's cinematic foot-

steps because Allen had so thoroughly mined both the genre and New York City on film. But for the most part, reviews were highly favorable, and during a season that offered such blockbusters as *Batman, Indiana Jones and the Last Crusade,* and *Lethal Weapon 2, When Harry Met Sally* provided adult moviegoers with a thoughtful, provocative alternative to the huge-budget action extravaganzas.

The positive reception did much to convince Reiner and Ephron of their sanity, for both have admitted that Harry and Sally were merely stand-ins for themselves. Their months of conversation had been an eye-opening journey into the dark heart of dating. Reiner had shocked Ephron with his frank revelations about the male psyche, and Ephron had likewise struck a sensitive chord with her confessions of female

shenanigans and the most prevalent of the female ruse—the orgasm.

Over the years, a slew of comedies have made light of that "special moment." Woody Allen's futuristic Orgasmatron device, for example, provided it on demand in *Sleeper* (1973). *There's Something About Mary* (1998) used it to introduce a bizarre new trend in hairstyling. And in *American Pie* (1999), the desire to attain it prompted a passionate encounter between a young man and a fruit-filled pastry. Needless to say, the subject presented fertile ground for parody.

First, the filmmakers had to set the record straight. During the course of writing the screenplay, when Ephron had ventured to say that it was common knowledge that many women feign orgasms during sex, Reiner was dumbfounded. The nonplussed director immediately decided to conduct a poll of his own and found to his surprise that more than 60 percent of the women he interviewed admitted to having "faked it." His perfectly ordered sexual universe crumbling around him, Reiner did what any true artist would: He used his disillusionment as material.

Shot at Katz's Deli on Manhattan's Lower East Side, the scene begins with Harry revealing to Sally his technique for skipping out on dates after sleeping with them. Disgusted by his callousness and amused at his bold claim that women overlooked his quick exits because he satisfied them sexually, Sally floats a provocative idea: Harry's paramours could be acting. Impossible, says Harry.

"How do you know?" she asks.

"Because I know," he replies confidently. "You don't think I can tell the difference?"

Assuming the matter has been settled, Harry returns to his pastrami sandwich, only to glance up a moment later as Sally begins to moan and run her fingers through her hair. "You okay?" he mumbles, as nearby patrons begin to glance in their direction.

It was Ryan's idea to play the fake orgasm scene in a crowded restaurant, but according to Reiner, her initial embarrassment resulted in a too-timid performance. He encouraged the actress to throw caution to the wind. The second take was better but still too restrained for the director, who decided to demonstrate for himself the wild abandon he was looking for out of Ryan.

Taking a seat across from Crystal, Reiner proceeded to give his version of the orgasm. Pounding the table with his fist, sweat pouring down his bald pate, the bearded, heavyset Reiner shuddered and bellowed his way through the simulation.

The ice broken, Ryan came closer to the mark on the third take—and the fourth, fifth, and sixth. Ephron, in what one hopes is hyperbole, said the filming of the scene went on for eight to ten hours, with Ryan clutching, groaning, screaming, and spasming through take after take until Reiner got exactly what he wanted. Crystal quipped that her performance was so convincing he was deliberately flubbing his lines just to hear her do it again.

The kicker, however, was the scene's final line, suggested by Crystal. As the scandalized diners stare in amazement at Sally, a waiter approaches a neighboring table to take an order. The female patron, played by Reiner's mother, Estelle, clearly impressed by the wanton passion she has just witnessed, gestures at Harry and Sally's table and says matter-of-factly, "I'll have what she's having." The bon mot got the biggest laugh of the film, and according to the director, audiences regularly roared until halfway through the following scene.

It was a lark, but the scene that resulted became the film's trademark, leaving audiences howling and inspiring a critic from one popular national magazine to suggest that the bit be given "a prime spot in the comedy time capsule."

When Harry Met Sally became a hit, grossing nearly $93 million, by far the biggest take of Reiner's career at the time, and served as a professional springboard for everyone involved. The film was nominated for five Golden Globe Awards and one Oscar.

In homage to the lasting influence of the film, Ephron tells the story that on a flight years later she requested a complicated meal full of substitutions, conditionals, and the like. The bewildered flight attendant looked at her in consternation and asked, "Have you ever seen that movie *When Harry Met Sally*?"

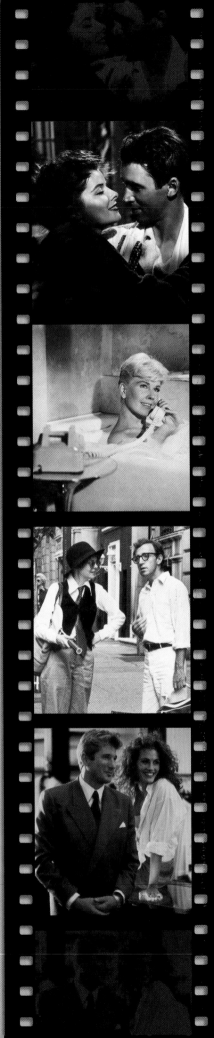

ROMANTIC COMEDIES

The "game of love" is at the heart of the plot of every great romantic comedy. Here are five classics from throughout motion picture history that played the game well.

The Philadelphia Story (1940) The wedding of high-society girl Tracy Lord (Katharine Hepburn) to stuffy coal-company executive George Kittredge (John Howard) promises to be the social event of the season. Lord's ex-husband, Dexter Haven (Cary Grant), crashes the festivities, bringing along fast-talking tabloid reporter Macaulay Connor (James Stewart). Connor falls for the beautiful Tracy, and with only hours before she's to walk down the aisle, the bride-to-be has three suitors vying for her affections. James Stewart won the Oscar for Best Actor. It was one of nine films George Cukor directed with Katharine Hepburn and one of the great romantic comedies from MGM's golden age.

Pillow Talk (1959) The famous Day-Hudson chemistry is never more present than in this, the first of their three highly successful romantic comedies. A Manhattan phone line shortage forces Jan Morrow (Doris Day) to share a party line on her home phone with playboy Brad Allen (Rock Hudson). Jan grows infuriated by the inordinate amount of time Brad ties up the line wooing his various girlfriends. In a convenient coincidence, Brad discovers that his old college pal Jonathan Forbes (Tony Randall) is dating Jan, and when they come face-to-face, Brad is smitten and decides to pursue Jan himself. To hide his real identity Brad pretends to be a Texan named Rex Stetson, complete with a charm-dripping southern drawl. The film's cleverness comes from the witty innuendo-laced dialogue and the cinematic effects of the split-screen phone conversations. It's what producer Martin Melcher, also Day's husband, described as "a clean sex comedy."

Annie Hall (1977) In this near self-portrait, Woody Allen plays Alvy Singer, a neurotic Jewish TV comedian living in Manhattan who falls in love with Annie, a WASPy Midwesterner played by Diane Keaton (whose real last name is Hall). This bittersweet comedy, which Allen originally wrote as a lighthearted murder mystery, follows the rise and fall of Singer's relationship with Annie. One of the film's funnier, more awkward moments takes place in Annie's apartment. Alvy and Annie are mired in self-consciousness as they struggle through a conversation, and subtitles appear on screen revealing their true thoughts. The movie captured the Oscar for Best Picture in 1977 and established Woody Allen as a serious screen artist.

Pretty Woman (1990) Initially written as a dark story of an old prostitute's final chance at finding love, director Garry Marshall reworked the script into a heartwarming romance between Vivian, a Hollywood hooker played by Julia Roberts, and wealthy industrialist Edward Lewis, played by Richard Gere. Over the course of their one-week date, both are transformed. But Vivian turns down Lewis's offer to make her his mistress. "I want more. I want the fairy tale." The fairy tale is realized in the movie's final scene when Lewis gallantly pulls up in his white stretch limo, a dozen roses clenched in his teeth. Ignoring his fear of heights, he climbs up the fire escape to profess his love to Vivian.

My Big Fat Greek Wedding (2002) It's a classic Cinderella story. Toula Portokalos (Nia Vardalos), a thirty-year-old unmarried, unattractive introvert from a tight-knit Greek family, decides to take charge of her life, gives herself a makeover, and falls in love with the guy of her dreams, Ian (John Corbett). One big problem—Ian's not Greek, and Toula's father considers any non-Greek a *xenos,* a foreigner. Their love is tested, and hilarity ensues as Toula's dream guy is immersed in the nightmare that is the lovingly overbearing Portokalos family. The constant ribbing that Ian takes from Toula's two very protective brothers, Nick (Louis Mandylor) and Angelo (Joey Fatone), is especially hilarious. When Ian's and Toula's families meet for the first time, Ian asks Nick how to say in Greek, "Everyone, let's go in the house." Only after shouting the phrase as Nick had instructed, *"Eho tria arhidia,"* does Ian discover to his embarrassment that he has announced to his future in-laws, "I have three testicles." *My Big Fat Greek Wedding* became the big fat sleeper hit of 2002.

FIELD OF DREAMS

1989

Baseball and the movies have enjoyed a close relationship through the years. That's true in part because of the game's larger-than-life heroes and inherent drama—victory can turn on every pitch and every at bat—but it's mostly because movies and baseball are where miracles happen. The game serves as a reminder of innocence and a metaphor for the revitalization of faded dreams and redemption, and it represents the sacred tether between a boy and his dad. Such is the role that baseball plays in *Field of Dreams*, writer-director Phil Alden Robinson's adaptation of W. P. Kinsella's novel *Shoeless Joe*.

Shoeless Joe was the movie's working title during filming, but studio executives insisted on a new title.

The alternatives included *Miracle Ray, Heaven Is Iowa,* and *Dad's Second Chance.* Finally, *Field of Dreams* was chosen. When Robinson called W. P. Kinsella to say *Shoeless Joe* had been dropped, Kinsella astonished him by saying that *Shoeless Joe* had been his publisher's idea—the author's original title was *Dream Field.*

Kevin Costner stars as Ray Kinsella, a city kid and child of the '60s who at thirty-six finds himself a husband, father, and Iowan farmer. Out of the blue one day, while walking in the middle of his cornfield, Ray hears a beckoning voice whispering, "If you build it, he will come." After much consternation over whether the mystical voice originated from his head or the heavens, Ray complies and

extraordinarily grateful and brings with him other long-dead ballplayers looking for a second chance.

Kinsella nearly loses his farm but keeps listening to the instructions of the voice, next trekking to Boston, where he ropes in a reclusive writer played by James Earl Jones, and to Minnesota, where he meets the ghost of an old doctor played by Burt Lancaster. Back in Iowa, Ray finally understands that his journey provided a chance to reach out to and reconnect with his deceased father.

Robinson made several crucial changes in adapting Kinsella's novel. He made Ray and his wife, Anni, played by Amy Madigan, initially skeptical of the voice. He even filmed a scene in which Ray gets his hearing checked, although it was cut from the film. In order to sharpen the father-son focus, Robinson also wrote that Ray's mother had passed away in his childhood. He humanized the ballplayers more—when Anni calls Ray in for dinner, the

plows under his cornfield to build a baseball diamond where the specter of "Shoeless" Joe Jackson, his father's idol who had been undone by scandal when he was accused of helping to throw the 1919 World Series, mysteriously appears. Jackson, played by Ray Liotta, is

players gently tease him, "Dinner, Raaaayyy"—and made Mark, the man trying to buy Ray's farm, less of a villain. In fact, in the film version Mark is Ray's well-intentioned but overly pragmatic brother-in-law.

The biggest change was made for legal reasons. In the book, the cynical, withdrawn author Ray tries to help is J. D. Salinger, but Salinger threatened lawsuits if he was portrayed on the screen. Robinson invented Terence Mann and struggled mightily with casting until he saw James Earl Jones in *Fences* on Broadway. He was struck by the image of Ray trying to kidnap a man with Jones's physical presence, and everything fell into place. He wrote Mann's part hoping Jones would accept the role.

Finding the actor to play Ray Kinsella, however, was the most important casting decision. Kevin Costner was at his peak, coming off such successful movies as *No Way Out, The Untouchables,* and another baseball-themed film, *Bull Durham.* Costner appealed to both men and women, and his well-grounded, rugged presence would make Ray's flights of fancy seem believable.

Even so, no one thought Costner would do a second straight baseball movie, and Robinson crossed Costner off his list. Then a Universal executive persuaded Costner to read the script, and the actor—despite protests from his handlers—decided he had to make the movie.

The other crucial decision was finding the right location. Robinson decided to shoot around Dubuque, Iowa, because the region was diverse enough to use for local scenes but could also double for the movie's other locations, Boston and Chisholm, Minnesota. The location scouts drove six hundred miles of country roads searching for the perfect farm—one with the right kind of farmhouse on a rise to provide good visuals but with enough flat land for a ball field. Near the town of

Dyersville, they finally found Don Lansing's house and farm, although left and center field would actually be set on his neighbor Al Ameskamp's property.

With Lansing's permission, the crew gutted his house, knocking down most interior walls to allow for camera movement and removing the upstairs ceiling to hang lights. Then they planted corn in the field. The production schedule was based on the corn's growth, so all interior shots were done first while the corn grew. The plan called for the corn to reach shoulder height by June 20, leaving just enough time to get all the shooting done before Costner had to leave for his next movie on August 15. But 1988 witnessed one of the region's worst droughts in memory, and the corn wasn't growing while the calendar pages turned. Robinson prepared to order fake corn, but instead, he dammed up the local creek, irrigated the field, and spent $25,000 trucking in water. It worked so well that Costner had to walk on raised planks in some scenes because the corn had grown so high.

Then it was time to plow the corn and build a baseball field. One hundred locals helped the crew do the work in two days, but there was no time to grow

grass, so they laid sod and continually painted it green during filming.

Working on location was rough on the actors—the heat was unbearable, the stench of nearby pig farms frequently hung in the air, and hordes of huge flies hovered about. Even filming at night was complicated—the ball field's lights attracted every bug in the vicinity and convinced the cows and roosters that it was daytime. The animals made so much noise that key dialogue had to be looped in later in a studio.

When the breaks fell Robinson's way, he was quick to capitalize. Bad weather interrupted shooting one day, so he captured amazing lightning strikes on film. Another day, a fog rolled in, and they used it to make Shoeless Joe's first appearance seem more mysterious.

While Costner was an accomplished athlete and most of the other "players" had minor-league or semipro experience, Liotta hadn't played much baseball. Legendary USC coach Rod Dedeaux and former Baltimore Oriole Don Buford worked with the cast, and when filming started, Liotta's skills had improved markedly. Although Jackson's home run was actually shot from a ball gun, the other hits were real. But the best moment

came about naturally—when Ray tells Shoeless Joe he's going to pitch a curve, Liotta just happened to slam the ball back up the middle, toppling Costner, who had the presence of mind to improvise a sheepish reaction.

The trickiest shot was the ending, which showed hundreds of cars driving to the field. Robinson had fifteen hundred locals drive their cars along the road, but because the long line moved so slowly, the shot wasn't working. For the final take, Robinson flew with a cameraman in a helicopter, and he sent a message to the local radio station that was broadcasting instructions to the drivers out of Lansing's farmhouse. He had all the drivers put their cars in park but flash their high beams on and off, which perfectly created the illusion of motion.

Before releasing the film, Robinson screened it for a test audience. In tallying the responses, he discovered a crucial oversight: Viewers were upset that at the end, Ray and his father never openly acknowledged they were father and son. So when Ray asks his dad, John Kinsella, "Want to have a catch?" Robinson looped in a phrase to make it, "Hey, Dad, want to have a catch?" That small change made all the difference.

Once the movie made it into theaters, audience reactions were split. Some critics assailed the sappiness, while others attacked the inaccuracies. Liotta batted right and threw left; in real life, Jackson did the opposite. Jackson was famous for his black bat and his laconic naïveté, which were conspicuously absent in the film. Still others were upset at the notion of romanticizing the eight ballplayers who fixed the 1919 World Series. But others swooned over the movie's mix of magic and heartfelt emotion. Critic Roger Ebert called it "visionary."

Despite the critical response, the movie became a tremendous hit, and the phrases "Field of Dreams" and "If you build it, he will come" entered the pop lexicon. In fact, when Lansing decided to leave the field intact after filming ended, people did indeed come. Ameskamp replanted corn on his portion but was so overwhelmed by angry notes that he rebuilt the baseball outfield the following year. Every year, thousands of people still travel to the baseball diamond in the Iowa cornfield hoping to catch some of its magic.

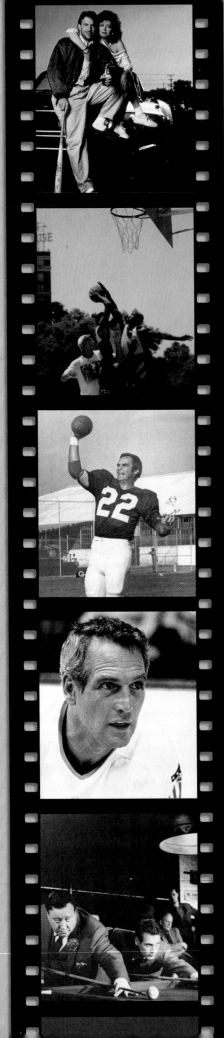

SPORTS MOMENTS

It's been said that sports is drama without a script. Here are some of the more unforgettable *scripted* sports moments.

Baseball

Bull Durham and **Eight Men Out** (1988) In one year, *Bull Durham* and *Eight Men Out* captured baseball's quirkiness and exuberance and revealed its potential for tragedy and heartbreak. The highlight of *Bull Durham* comes when dimwitted lunk Nuke LaLoosh dons garters, begins breathing through his eyelids, and suddenly starts pitching like an ace. *Eight Men Out,* the story of the fixing of the 1919 World Series, has even better baseball action, especially when White Sox third baseman Buck Weaver (John Cusack) makes sterling defensive plays. But the most poignant scene is the sepia-toned final shots of Joe Jackson, banned from professional ball, playing his heart out in semipro obscurity just for the love of the game.

Basketball

White Men Can't Jump (1992) *Hoosiers* has the inspirational script and speeches, but when it comes to on-court action in all it's trash-talking, elbow-throwing, hard-to-the hoop glory, this film has got game. The two-on-two tournament is riveting, but what street hustlers Billy (Woody Harrelson) and Sidney (Wesley Snipes) try to pull off may be even more dynamic. Then again, this movie makes even a shoot-out contest compelling, with taunts that range from foul-mouthed to poetic—one character heckles by quoting John Keats. And it counts.

Football

The Longest Yard (1974) Burt Reynolds is Paul Crewe, a former pro quarterback disgraced in a point-shaving scandal who later finds himself in prison. He's asked by the warden to lead a team of convicts against the prison guards, but he's also told to throw the game. The play is unthinkably violent but the most memorable moment is Reynolds's last-minute quarterback scramble for the end zone and redemption.

Hockey

Slap Shot (1977) It's hockey, so naturally the most memorable scenes involve fights. The story follows a ragtag minor-league team inspired to greatness by their bloodlust after player-coach Reg Dunlop (Paul Newman) instigates them. The high point comes when he lets loose the geeky Hanson brothers for the first time and watches as they're instantly transformed from end-of-the-bench loons to head-thwacking goons.

Golf

Caddyshack (1980) "He's the Cinderella boy." When crazed groundskeeper Carl Spackler, played by Bill Murray, tees off on his flowers while announcing his fantasy triumph at Augusta, it takes the elitist golf clubs down a peg and captures the frustrations of the amateur golfer and the improvisational genius of Murray all in one scene.

Pool

The Hustler (1961) Mixing the focused intensity of a duel with the staggering endurance required of a marathon, the matchup between two supremely confident men—insolent upstart Fast Eddie (Paul Newman) and undefeated champ Minnesota Fats (Jackie Gleason)—is a classic in mano a mano competition. That the game of pool also moves the story along and reveals insights into the major characters makes it a classic in moviemaking.

THE SILENCE OF THE LAMBS

1991

In his 1981 novel *Red Dragon,* author Thomas Harris introduced readers to one of the most fiendish characters in modern fiction: Dr. Hannibal Lecter, a brilliant psychiatrist–turned–psychopathic–serial killer, nicknamed Hannibal "the Cannibal" for his gruesome ritual of dining on the remains of his victims.

Harris made Lecter a central figure again in his 1988 psychological thriller, *The Silence of the Lambs,* the brutal and intensely disturbing story of the rampage of a serial killer, Jame Gumb, known to detectives as "Buffalo Bill" for the way he skins his victims. Clarice Starling, a young, ambitious FBI trainee, is sent to interrogate Lecter in prison in hopes that she can gain

insight into the mind of a madman and help the FBI nab the at-large murderer.

The book became a national best-seller and actor Gene Hackman and Orion Pictures snapped up the rights for Hackman to star in and direct the film. When Hackman read an early version of screenwriter Ted Tally's script, however, he decided the movie was too grisly and sold his interest back to Orion. Hackman was not the only person in Hollywood to be put off by the film's horrifying subject matter.

To keep the project alive, Orion next offered the film to director Jonathan Demme, although Demme's movies like *Married to the Mob* and *Melvin and*

Howard seemed drastically different in tone from *Lambs*. Demme also declined, telling then-head of Orion Pictures Mike Medavoy he wasn't interested in doing a "slasher" film. Medavoy persisted, urging Demme to read the book. He complied and was struck by the dimension of the characters and "the complicated and interesting themes," and Demme agreed to take on the project.

Medavoy's choice for the role of Lecter was Robert Duvall. However, Demme preferred lesser-known British actor Anthony Hopkins, impressed by his humane performance in *The Elephant Man*. "What really counts is the ability to convey humanity and intelligence," Demme once said of the part of Lecter. "Lecter is insidious, and that's where the terror arises—from the distortion of humanity and intelligence."

Hopkins was initially leery of the role, but after reading the script for *Lambs* he immediately knew two things: This incarnation of Lecter was a once-in-a-lifetime role, and he knew exactly how to play him.

Hopkins said later that what he understood first about Lecter was his voice. "It had to be detached, dis-

embodied," Hopkins said. "So I took the computer voice of HAL from Stanley Kubrick's *2001*—cold, mechanical, exact. Terrifying." When he was about to read for Medavoy, a friend asked Hopkins if he was prepared, and he responded by uttering the now-famous greeting, "Hello, Clareeece."

For Starling, Demme originally wanted *Married to the Mob* star Michelle Pfeiffer. However, Pfeiffer, like Hackman, was repulsed by the violence and rejected the role. Meanwhile, Jodie Foster campaigned for the part, and her sturdiness and determination won Demme over.

When he arrived on the set, Hopkins—who did no research for his role—had already marked up his script with nuances about Lecter's dress, walk, smile, talk, laughter, and even his slicked-back hair. One of the actor's notes described the character as "fit and fierce as a caged panther."

In contrast, Foster immersed herself in research, doing several days of intensive training at the FBI Academy in Quantico, Virginia, and studying insects at the Smithsonian to understand the death's-head moths that became a pivotal clue in the film. The FBI, which

viewed *Lambs* as a chance to recruit female agents, was extremely cooperative, even allowing filming at Quantico. Scott Glenn's character of agent Jack Crawford was based on real FBI behavioral scientist John Douglass, who consulted on the film.

Demme chose to film *Lambs* primarily in and around Pittsburgh. The architecture and topography, with its surrounding hills, rivers, and nearby towns, allowed it to serve as many of the locales in Tally's screenplay, from the Baltimore psychiatric prison where Lecter was housed to Washington, D.C., Memphis, and the rural West Virginia town of Starling's childhood.

Meticulous attention was paid to every detail of the sets and costumes. Lecter's muzzling mask, which he was made to wear at his airport meeting with the dis-

tressed Senator Ruth Martin, went through several transformations, including one that looked like it belonged on a medieval liege man and one resembling the meshed hood worn while fencing. Finally, costumers settled on a fiberglass skin mask that covered the lower half of Hopkins's face, leaving his eyes, ears, and forehead exposed. The plan was to paint it, but it was decided that the raw leathery texture and metal bars running vertically across the opening for the mouth enhanced Lecter's monstrous aura.

An abandoned factory served as the state institution and housed the gothic-looking cellblock where Lecter was caged. Demme was frustrated at the prospect of shooting through traditional cell bars, believing it would be problematic for cinematographer

Tak Fujimoto and too distracting for his actors and the audience. Production designer Kristi Zea came up with the idea of replacing the bars with a thick wall of Plexiglas, the kind found in liquor stores and bank-teller windows. The thick, reinforced Plexiglas seemed a formidable cage wall for Lecter, while leaving the director and the actors unencumbered.

The four blood-chilling discussions between Lecter and Starling would become the heart of the movie; their first encounter was the most memorable. It begins with Starling cautiously walking down the long dingy corridor, lined on one side with barred dungeon-like prison cells, passing one deranged prisoner after another until she arrives at the windowless Plexiglas cage housing the notorious Dr. Lecter.

Starling's preconceived notions of the evil, violent psychopath are betrayed when she sees Lecter for the first time, standing, waiting respectfully in the center of his cell, with what Hopkins described as "reptilian-like stillness."

Lecter fixes his steel-blue eyes on Starling and offers a "Good morning," in a courteous yet contemptuous tone. The scene is taut as the two begin to spar. In spite of Lecter's condescending remarks and insults, Starling pushes on, hoping to elicit his insights into the personality of Buffalo Bill. Lecter, the predatory monster rendered incapable of inflicting physical harm, persists at dissecting Starling's personality with his brilliant, razor-sharp intellect.

The scene is seared into film history when Lecter reminds Starling of who he is and what he's capable of doing: "A census taker once tried to test me. I ate his liver with some fava beans and a nice Chianti." Lecter then makes a sinister sifting sound through his teeth, and backs away from the glass, leaving Starling dazed and the audience mesmerized.

Hopkins threw in the evil slurping as a joke. He was sure Demme would edit it out. Although Demme agreed that it was "over the top," he loved it and kept it in the film.

The prison scenes between Foster and Hopkins were arduous to film. The challenge was making a compelling scene out of two people just talking to each other. Demme shot them from different points of view and at a number of different angles. He integrated Hitchcock-like close-up techniques, at one point shooting Foster through Lecter's glass prison wall and reflecting Hopkins's image next to hers. For his part, Hopkins said that he didn't play up Lecter's evilness but rather his humanity, "the other side of his nature, the humor, the seductiveness, the wit, the perceptiveness. By playing those qualities," Hopkins insisted, "the audience does the work for you."

Another challenge for Demme and his crew involved the moths that Buffalo Bill left tucked in his victims' throats as a clue. The script called for death's-head moths, which come from Asia and have markings resembling a skull and crossbones on their backs. Insect wrangler Raymond Mendez was unable to import them, so he substituted three hundred tobacco horn worm moths, fitting a few of them with body shields that had the markings of the death's-head painted on them. The moths were flown in from the University of North Carolina and kept in a heat- and humidity-controlled room. They weren't brought onto the too-cold set until the last possible minute. The fake pupa chrysalis pulled out of a victim's throat was made of Tootsie Rolls, gummy bears, saffron, and oregano to achieve the right color and consistency.

Much of *Lamb*'s magic came in editing and post-production. Great care was taken not to cheapen the movie, so the music and sound effects were often underplayed. In the scene in which Starling uncovers a decapitated head in an abandoned storage facility, for example, Demme made sure to tone down the score so it would not signal to the audience that something shocking was coming.

Perhaps the most significant feature in terms of building tension was Demme's editing of the hunt for Buffalo Bill. Initially, the SWAT team's mistaken ambush of an abandoned house and Starling's confrontation with Gumb at an entirely different location were edited sequentially. Demme, again showing Hitchcock's influence, heightened the tension by intercutting them as parallel scenes.

The Silence of the Lambs was released on Valentine's Day 1991. The *New York Times* called it "pop filmmaking of a high order," and prophetically predicted, "It could very well be the first big hit of the year." The movie became only the third in Hollywood history to capture Oscars for Best Picture, Best Director, Best Actor, Best Actress, and Best Screenplay.

In 2003, the American Film Institute designated Dr. Hannibal "the Cannibal" Lector as the most terrifying villain in film history, capping a list of extraordinary achievements for a film many in Hollywood considered too gruesome to make.

MOVIE VILLAINS

In the movies, a hero can't be great without a great villain. There is no reason to cheer for heroes unless some person or entity puts obstacles in their way placing life, family, country, or their world in jeopardy. A hero needs something to bump up against, and the badder the bumper, the better the tale. In film, the villain is the character you love to hate. Although the American Film Institute named Hannibal Lecter the number one villain among their 100 Greatest Heroes and Villains, the list of great villains certainly doesn't end with him.

NURSE RATCHED in **One Flew Over the Cuckoo's Nest** (1975) A "wolf in sheep's clothing," the villainess Nurse Mildred Ratched is anything but the compassionate caregiver that her uniform would suggest. Louise Fletcher accepted the part of the domineering authoritarian only a week before cameras were to start rolling after five other actresses turned it down. As Jack Nicholson's antiheroic character Randle Patrick McMurphy struggles to bring life and sanity to the sterile and regimented hospital ward, he is thwarted at every turn by his emasculating, controlling archenemy Nurse Ratched.

DARTH VADER in the **Star Wars** saga (1977, 1980, 1983) Darth Vader is smart, twisted, and complex. He's gone over to the dark side and isn't above slicing off his own son's hand to prove a point. The sinister, helmeted mystery man with the mile-deep voice is someone who's been tempted by evil and succumbed—a villain made all the more dangerous by the complexity of his motives and the depth of his pain.

T-1000 in **Terminator II: Judgment Day** (1991) A villain doesn't have to be devious, brilliant, or twisted to be effective; he doesn't even have to be human. Robert Patrick plays the T-1000, a killing machine whose absolute lack of human qualities makes it a great villain. The T-1000's single-minded pursuit of John Connor and its seeming indestructibility make it one of the most effective foes in the movies. When the T-1000 emerges from a flaming truck crash that would have destroyed anyone human and reconstitutes its silvery self, the audience knows they're in for a thrill ride on a new level.

AMON GOETH in **Schindler's List** (1993) The villain is human, but one who might as well be a machine. Amon Goeth, the Nazi camp commander played by Ralph Fiennes, is a ruthless, sadistic psychopath who indiscriminately shoots prisoners for sport. The fact that the character was historical rather than fictional made Fiennes's portrayal all the more persuasive and horrifying. He embodied the evil that was the Third Reich and became one of movies' most hateful and despicable villains.

THELMA & LOUISE

1991

Thelma & Louise occupies a unique position in the history of film—it was the very first movie of the "outlaw buddy" genre in which the outlaw buddies were women. When the movie opened in 1991, it struck a nerve in its portrayal of female empowerment as it had never before been shown in a movie.

In the course of their four-day run from the law, the female fugitives are transformed, stripping away layers of societal convention to realize their true identities as women and as human beings. Director Ridley Scott described the film as "a hero's journey"; it wasn't intended to be a female manifesto or a male-bashing movie, but it was interpreted as both.

Screenwriter Callie Khouri and the film's stars, Susan Sarandon and Geena Davis, admit to being completely unprepared for the uproar generated by *Thelma & Louise.* Within a week of its release, Sarandon and Davis were on the cover of *Time,* and the critics lined up to praise and condemn the movie. Some of the criticism was brutal. John Leo of *U.S. News and World Report* wrote, "This is a quite small-minded, extremely toxic film, about as morally and intellectually screwed up as Hollywood can get." *Thelma & Louise* was decried for its violence against men, but in actuality, only three people die—the rapist and Thelma and Louise.

Director Ridley Scott, whose background was primarily in television commercials, estimated that he'd shot over 2,500 TV ads before he shot his first movie. The director of *Alien* and the noir sci-fi classic *Blade Runner*, Scott is known as one of film's top visual stylists, and he brought a painter's sensibility to *Thelma & Louise*.

Though set in Arkansas and the southwest, most of *Thelma & Louise* was shot in Southern California. The scenes where the two women drive through vast flat landscapes were actually filmed in farmland around Bakersfield, California. The breathtaking vista scenes, however, took place in Moab, Utah, the same backdrop used in the 1948 John Wayne Western *Fort Apache*. And the final scene, in which Thelma and Louise rocketed off a cliff in their airborne vintage Thunderbird, is located at the bottom end of the Grand Canyon.

Thelma & Louise was also a significant film in the careers of its costars Sarandon and Davis, and it provided a breakthrough role for Brad Pitt. Screenwriter Khouri recalls that when she first met Pitt on the set, she was so dazzled by him she was struck virtually speechless. The only word she managed to get out was, "Perfect."

Pitt's charming cowboy con man, J. D., was another example of the movie's use of role reversals. In the steamy motel scene with Thelma, Pitt was the sex object, not Davis. In fact, the actress remembers feigning irritation that Ridley Scott himself, as always seeking the perfect visual image, personally sprayed Pitt, not her, with Evian water before his takes so he would look flawless.

As the production drew closer to the scene between Davis and Pitt, Scott hedged his bets. On the chance that Davis would balk at the nudity required, he auditioned a string of actresses as body doubles. That is, until Davis caught wind of it. She promptly pulled the director aside and told him "Goddammit, Ridley, nobody's doubling my body!" It was Davis and Pitt in every shot.

When it came to casting, Scott always had his eye out for "local color," and he often added people to his movie that he met while filming. The line-dancers in the Silver Bullet Bar, for example, were real bar patrons. Scott included their rendition of the "Tush Push" in the movie after he'd seen them practicing the dance between takes. The old man Louise gives her watch and jewelry to was a ninety-two-year old former uranium miner who'd quit his trade just five years earlier. A cyclist Scott had seen on location inspired the Rasta biker who treats the locked-up state trooper to a puff from his giant spliff.

When it came to the fiery showdown between Thelma and Louise and the crude, obnoxious trucker, it was a big production complete with more than a half dozen cameras, including one mounted overhead on a helicopter. But a nervous Susan Sarandon noticed that although they'd cleared out everyone for three miles around, the actresses were within a hundred yards of the explosion.

Cameras were aimed at their backs but not their faces. So when Sarandon questioned Scott about the need for her and Davis to be so close, Ridley was inspired to set up two more cameras to capture their genuine reactions. When the actual explosion was set off, Sarandon and Davis were so awed by the pyrotechnics they forgot to "act." Their close-ups had to be reshot for "proper" reactions.

Of all the memorable moments in *Thelma & Louise*, the one that perhaps best represents the movie is the final scene, in which the women make the decision that they're never turning back—to face the law or their former lives. The ending was shot, appropriately, in the final hour of the final day. Scott says, "[It was]

all shot in desperately short time—we did all this in about forty-five minutes. If I'd gone another day, it would have been a four-day weekend that would have cranked the budget up another six or seven hundred thousand dollars. I knew I had to get it then."

So with the sun low in the sky, it came time to shoot the approach to the cliff. Scott, who did much of the photography on the movie, was in the backseat filming; Davis sat in the passenger seat; and a female stunt driver steered toward the canyon's edge. Scott told Davis that if there was an accident, he'd die with her.

Scott then shot one of Hollywood's most memorable scenes: the image of the Thunderbird frozen in flight over the Grand Canyon with Thelma and Louise

choosing the "freedom" of death. With literally moments of daylight left, two very lifelike dummies resembling Thelma and Louise, with proper expressions fixed on their faces, were strapped into the bucket seats of the Thunderbird. As Scott called "Action!" a bank of cameras rolled, and the remote-controlled convertible made its journey off the edge of the cliff and into film immortality. Scott had his fingers crossed, and was overjoyed at the T-Bird's trajectory: "Thank God the car didn't spin or roll or somersault—I wanted that car to continue as if it were still driving."

Davis remembers, "After we did the second take, Ridley said 'Cut!' And boop! There went the sun. It was just like a movie."

Unlike the cut in the finished movie with the T-Bird frozen in midair, an alternate ending showed the car as it arced downward into the canyon. This visual was too disturbing—much too final—for test audiences and it was summarily rejected. Scott refers to the chosen ending as the "happy" ending.

When the movie was screened at the Cannes Film Festival, Geena Davis thought they had a flop on their hands. For the first ten minutes of the movie, there was no audience reaction at all. Everyone was stone silent. But when Louise shot the rapist in the parking lot, the audience erupted in cheers. From then on, Davis knew they were okay.

Oscar time rolled around, and Ridley Scott was

nominated for Best Director and Susan Sarandon and Geena Davis were both nominated for Best Actress. Adrian Biddle was nominated for his photography, and Thom Noble his editing. But the only Academy Award the film won went to Callie Khouri for Best Writing, Screenplay Written Directly for the Screen.

Thelma & Louise took audiences down a highway rarely traveled, a journey to the crossroads where social commentary and entertainment met to produce a movie that is both enlightening and enchanting, and totally unforgettable.

Unforgettable
BUDDY MOVIES

Buddy movies cross several genres. There are comedy buddy movies, action buddy movies, and cop buddy movies. In many cases, the "buddies" aren't really pals—they're thrown together by circumstance and are often at each other's throats. But it doesn't matter whether it's silly slapstick, grand adventure, or gritty action, it takes great stars and great chemistry to create true classics. Here are some of Hollywood's more popular pairings.

The Road to Morocco (1942) Bob Hope and Bing Crosby are such charming schemers in their four *Road* movies that you don't mind the lack of sensible plot. Their relationship always crackles with lighthearted tension, and their comic delivery is tops. In *Morocco*, they're stranded on a raft in the ocean when Crosby starts musing about eating Hope. "You mean you'd eat me . . . without vegetables?" Hope retorts. "You wouldn't like me. Once I bit my tongue and I tasted terrible." They soon find land, where they're each surreptitiously kissed by a camel.

The Defiant Ones (1958) In the early years of the civil rights movement, this interracial buddy movie made a powerful statement. Johnny Jackson (Tony Curtis) and Noah Cullen (Sidney Poitier) are escaped convicts who must learn to get along because they are shackled to each other. In the memorable climax, Cullen jumps aboard a freight train and reaches back to pull Jackson up—the image of the black and white arms locked together is indelible, as is the finale when Cullen can't save Jackson and sacrifices his own freedom, falling back to the ground with his friend to await capture.

The Producers (1968) Zero Mostel as Max Bialystock and Gene Wilder as Leo Bloom make every moment a funny one. Among the highlights are their promenade through the park—when they ride a carousel and rent a boat together—and their panicked fight over the cooked books after these two Broadway producers realize the flop they had hoped for is going to be a huge hit. Ali-Frasier, it's not.

The Odd Couple (1968) Before Tony Randall and Jack Klugman on TV came Jack Lemmon and Walter Matthau in the best of their many pairings together. Two divorced men, the neurotically neat Felix Ungar (Lemmon) and the ultraslob Oscar Madison (Matthau), must learn to live together, but they fight over everything along the way. In one vintage argument, know-it-all Felix corrects Oscar in the kitchen saying, "It's not spaghetti, it's linguini." Oscar hurls the linguini at the wall, replying, "Now it's garbage." And don't expect him to clean it up.

BUDDY MOVIES CONTINUED

Butch Cassidy and the Sundance Kid (1969) This is the quintessential American buddy movie with the quintessential American movie stars. Paul Newman and Robert Redford star as the lovable rogues looking to move from the American West to Bolivia for a new opportunity. Moviedom's best buddy scene comes when they're trapped at a cliff's edge, over-looking rushing water. Sundance confesses, "I can't swim." Butch laughs and says, "Why, you're crazy, the fall'll probably kill ya," and off the ledge they leap, shouting "Awww, s——-t!" as they go.

The Man Who Would Be King (1975) Danny Dravot (Sean Connery) and Peachy Carnehan (Michael Caine) are England's answer to Butch and Sundance. Connery and Caine have the charm and charisma to match Newman and Redford in this rollicking adventure classic and sly political satire. Danny and Peachy are British soldiers at the height of the British Empire. They con the priests of remote Kafiristan into believing Danny is a god who should be made king of the land, and the finale here equals Butch and Sundance's Bolivian shootout: When Danny is revealed to be merely human, he's forced to march on a wooden bridge over a canyon. The bridge's ropes are cut, and he plummets down, but before he goes, he and Peachy share one last moment together, singing loudly and joyfully in the face of death.

48 Hrs. (1982) This raw and raucous gem helped spark a trend, inspiring a slew of mostly inferior cop/buddy/action movies, including the more polished and popular *Lethal Weapon* series. Jack Cates (Nick Nolte) is a temperamental detective who springs smooth-talking Reggie Hammond (Eddie Murphy) from jail to track down a cop killer. The two dislike each other instantly, and when Reggie overreaches with a comment about partnership, Jack snarls, "We ain't partners, we ain't brothers, and we ain't friends." It's a memorable scene made more so when Jack, having softened a bit (he has called Reggie everything from "watermelon" to "spear chucker") uses the word "partner," and Reggie throws Jack's line right back in his face.

Midnight Run (1988) The explosive Jack Walsh (Robert De Niro) is a bounty hunter forced to drag whiny accountant Jonathan Mardukas (Charles Grodin) across the country to jail where he'll almost definitely be killed by the mob boss whose money he embezzled. (Mardukas gave most of the money to charity.) Chased by the FBI, the Mafia, and another bounty hunter, the two bicker and battle the entire way. Finally, aboard a freight train out west, Mardukas, who has been hoping to persuade Walsh to free him, says quietly, "Under other circumstance, you and I . . . probably would still have hated each other." Walsh laughs, then turns sincere and says they might have been friends, actually.

PULP FICTION

1994

The mantra of screenwriters in Hollywood is "Write something familiar—but with a twist." Quentin Tarantino took that mantra, wrote a script with some of the most familiar elements in movie history, and twisted them in ways that made them totally original, uncomfortably disturbing, and completely entertaining.

Much as the Lucas-Spielberg collaboration on Indiana Jones was an homage to, and an update of, the adventure serials of the 1940s, *Pulp Fiction* pays tribute to 1970s films—especially those of French "New Wave" auteurs like Jean-Luc Godard, François Truffaut, and Jean-Pierre Melville. These were filmmakers who prided themselves on the use of unconventional camera techniques, nonlinear storytelling, and lengthy stretches of dialogue.

Tarantino's genius was a mixture of his encyclopedic knowledge of movies, his love of them, and his equally impressive knowledge of popular culture. *Pulp Fiction* is chock-full of cultural and film references that are sometimes obvious, sometimes obscure, and yet always clever.

Equally important to Tarantino was his choice of music. In fact, the director has said that without the music, there is no movie. He picks approximately 60 percent of the songs he wants to include before he even begins to write a script, another 20 percent are chosen while he's writing, and the rest while shooting or in postproduction. And those choices are always eclectic and fresh.

The music throughout *Pulp Fiction* comes from a wide range of genres and generations: "Jungle Boogie" by Kool and the Gang, "Lonesome Town" by Ricky Nelson, "Son of a Preacher Man" by Dusty Springfield, "Flowers on the Wall" by the Statler Brothers, "Let's Stay Together" by Al Green, and Tarantino's inspired choice for the twist contest, "You Never Can Tell" by Chuck Berry.

"Misirlou" is the first song heard in *Pulp Fiction* and became the movie's de facto theme. To Tarantino, Dick Dale's legendary surf guitar song is a masterpiece, a theme befitting the likes of "*The Good, The Bad, and the Ugly* [and] *Ben Hur*. It's very heraldic."

When it came time to cast the movie, he was equally clever. He reached back to the 1970s for one of his favorite cultural icons who had lost his glitter— John Travolta. A star of the highest magnitude in the

1970s and '80s, Travolta had watched his career devolve. He was still working, making good money with his *Look Who's Talking* trilogy, but his hipness factor was near zero. Tarantino and *Pulp Fiction* resurrected him. After portraying low-rent but charming hit man Vincent Vega, the one-time Sweathog of *Welcome Back, Kotter* fame and star of *Saturday Night Fever* shot back to the head of the class, soon becoming one of Hollywood's highest-paid leading men.

To play Jules, Travolta's Bible-verse spouting partner in crime, Tarantino picked actor Samuel L. Jackson. Uma Thurman was cast as Mia Wallace, the temptress wife of Vincent and Jules's notorious gangster-boss Marsellus Wallace, who was played by Ving Rhames. And to complete the casting in *Pulp Fiction*'s three intersecting stories, Tarantino chose action-adventure star Bruce Willis.

Willis was already one of Hollywood's biggest rough-and-tumble heroes, but his low-key portrayal of conflicted boxer Butch Coolidge introduced audiences to a whole new dimension of the *Die Hard* hero.

The characters of Vincent and Jules are formally introduced to the audience on their early morning ride to what we discover is the assassination of a foursome of college types who have double-crossed their crime partner, Marsellus Wallace. The black-suited pals are cold-blooded professional killers, but surprisingly, their conversation isn't shoptalk. Quentin Tarantino says, "They're on their way to blow away a couple of guys. But the thing is, they're just going to work. So they're having, like, a carpool conversation."

It's that lengthy conversation that sets up the rest of the movie. The audience discovers that this is no ordinary crime drama—the dialogue is very natural and, at the same time, unconventional, dark, and funny. The most memorable part of the exchange takes place in the car. Vincent has just returned from Europe where he has encountered a French outpost of McDonald's. He regales Jules with the differences between the Paris and American versions of the chain's various hamburgers. While the "Big Mac" is simply "Le Big Mac" Jules seems most impressed that the metric system has forced Parisians to rename the Quarter Pounder a "Royale with cheese."

Pulp Fiction's sharp dialogue was just one of its engaging elements. It also had frightening, unnerving scenes like the one in which Mia accidentally overdoses on Vincent's super-potent heroin. Tarantino was determined to get this powerful scene perfect. In it, Vincent knows that if Mia dies, his own life is over because his

boss, Marsellus, is her husband. With Mia comatose in the front seat of his car, Vincent speeds to the home of the smarmy drug dealer, Lance, played by Eric Stoltz, who sold him the super smack.

The only thing Lance can suggest is to give Mia a shot of adrenalin, "straight into the heart." After the huge hypodermic needle is prepared, Vince is given the task of administering it, with the admonition that he has to stab the needle in with enough force to penetrate Mia's chest wall. After marking the insertion point with a red felt-tip marker, Vince rears back and pounds the needle into Mia's chest, causing her to spring back to life and gasp for air.

The filmmakers were afraid that if Travolta actually hit Thurman in the chest with the necessary force, it could easily have broken her ribs. So in order to make the scene as believable as possible, John Travolta was

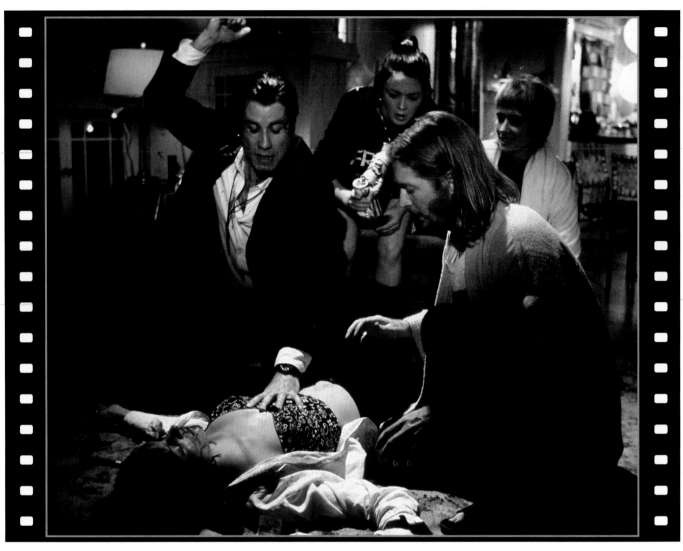

actually filmed pulling the retractable needle out of Uma Thurman's chest. The scene was reversed in editing, creating the desired illusion. In real life, adrenalin is not an antidote for a heroin overdose, and no needle, no matter how sharp, would penetrate a person's chest wall without bending. But for the purposes of the movie, the high-tension scene that Tarantino concocted was incredibly effective.

The adrenalin scene was so powerful, in fact, that during the film's American debut at the New York Film Festival, one audience member passed out. The event assured a new level of appreciation for the movie, not to mention increased its mystique.

Pulp Fiction debuted at the Cannes Film Festival and earned Quentin Tarantino its highest award, the Palme D'Or. In America, it was nominated for seven Academy Awards and won one—Tarantino and Roger Avary picked up the Oscar for Best Writing, Screenplay Written Directly for the Screen.

However, *Pulp Fiction* did more than win awards that year; it reinvented a genre. It has been the progenitor to dozens of dark, twisted, funny movies that, in deference to the former video store clerk who directed it, have almost always been referred to as "Tarantino-like" or "Tarantinoesque." Few have equaled it. Although the movie has become the visual definition of *pulp fiction*—containing lurid subject matter and being characteristically printed on rough, unfinished paper—it has become one of America's most distinctive and intelligent films.

WHAT'S IN THE BRIEFCASE?

It has become one of the great-unanswered movie mysteries: What exactly were the glowing contents in the briefcase in *Pulp Fiction*? Quentin Tarantino says there is no official explanation, and he told Travolta, "It is whatever you want it to be." Whatever it was, it was so beautiful that people were willing to kill for it. The ambiguity helped fuel the cult legend of the film. Here are some of the more plausible, popular, and preposterous theories.

THE SOUL OF MARCELLUS WALLACE One theory suggests that mobster Marcellus Wallace has sold his soul to the devil, but the deal's gone bad and Wallace wants it back. Wallace's henchmen, Vincent and Jules, recover the briefcase in an early morning ambush of some of the devil's crew. Before leaving Vincent checks the contents. The devilish combination "666" springs the lock and, as Vincent lifts the lid, a "heavenly" glow emanates from the case. Just as Vincent and his partner are about to make their escape, a man bursts in from another room with his gun blazing. To everyone's amazement, not a single bullet finds its intended target, which Jules reverentially attributes to "divine intervention." God was protecting those with the lost soul.

AN HOMAGE TO ALFRED HITCHCOCK The master of suspense was renowned for his insertion of a plot device in his movies that really was nothing more than an entertaining distraction, something the audience thinks is important but really isn't. He called such devices MacGuffins, and the theory is that Tarantino used the briefcase as a MacGuffin-like thread woven throughout his otherwise non-linear story.

TWO LIGHTS AND SOME BATTERIES Ignoring the mystical meaning of the glow from the briefcase, Samuel L. Jackson (Jules) offered his very practical perspective in a 1995 *Playboy* interview: "When I looked inside, between scenes, I saw two lights and some batteries. What I would have wanted to see are the next ten films I'm going to do and hope they're all as good as *Pulp Fiction*."

OTHER SUNDRY THEORIES The *Toronto Star* conducted a poll inviting readers to offer their ideas about what was contained in the briefcase. Here are their more popular responses: the Oscar that Tarantino hoped to win, O. J.'s other glove, Michael Jackson's other glove, or the diamonds from the robbery in Tarantino's *Reservoir Dogs*. The winning suggestion theorized that it was all an homage to Robert Aldrich's film *Kiss Me Deadly*, which featured a briefcase "glowing" from the nuclear bomb hidden inside.

THERE'S SOMETHING ABOUT MARY

1998

The 1990s was a decade of political incorrectness in comedies. Film-makers continually pushed the envelope of pure absurdity, and audiences responded. Brothers Peter and Bobby Farrelly were a particularly powerful creative force behind the trend of making taste-less subjects palatable.

These two irreverent directors are to filmmaking what shock jocks are to radio. Their 1994 movie, *Dumb and Dumber,* marked their first major success in feature comedy and proved that crude toilet humor sells. The 1996 film *Kingpin,* starring Woody Harrelson and Bill Murray, included a scene in which a prosthetic hand gets stuck in a bowling ball as it tumbles down the lane, again affirming that lowbrow comedy was a hot ticket at the box office.

After putting the fin-ishing touches on *King-pin,* the brothers came across a story written by TV writers Ed Decter and John Strauss with an age-old plotline about a young man trying to rekindle the flame of a former heartthrob. In a collaborative effort, the Far-rellys punched up the story with their emblematic brand of repulsive yet compelling humor.

The result was the raucous and raunchy comedy *There's Something About Mary,* in which the Farrelly

brothers did more than just ride the wave of vulgarity; they broke new ground in the comedy genre. They poked fun at previously taboo subjects, reviving classic elements of slapstick to make one of the most tasteless yet touching comedies in a generation.

Ben Stiller was cast as lovestruck suitor Ted Stroehmann, who can't forget the girl of his high school dreams, Mary Matthews, played by Cameron Diaz. Ted is an awkward klutz, a homely geek with a mouthful of braces. He's an unlikely match for the beautiful, alluring Mary, who embodies all the ideal traits of the "perfect girl"—sweet, outgoing, and graceful. But sixteen-year-old Mary discovers her soft spot for Ted when he defends her mentally challenged younger brother against a high school bully.

In the first plot twist, Mary rewards Ted's chivalry by asking him to take her to the senior prom. When Ted arrives to pick Mary up, he learns the hard way

that Mary's mentally handicapped brother, Warren, convincingly portrayed by W. Earl Brown, has a phobia about his ears. Giving him a baseball as a present, and pretending to "magically" pull the baseball from behind Warren's ear, Ted is immediately attacked by the bulky, childlike teenager. Stiller, who performed all his own stunts in the film, learned the hard way that Brown was committed to making his role entirely realistic. He lifted Stiller into the air like a professional wrestler and sent him crashing to the hardwood floor.

Ted's violent fall sets up the film's first memorable scene, when he excuses himself to use the bathroom. In his haste to zip up his fly, Ted unfortunately manages to get his "family jewels" caught in his zipper and lets out a bloodcurdling scream. The Farrellys made this perversely embarrassing moment completely hilarious by employing the traditional slapstick construction of bringing one character after another into the scene.

The scene is classically choreographed, as Mary's stepdad, Charlie, is the first to venture into the bathroom to see what the problem is. He's stupefied; Charlie just can't understand. "How the hell did you get the beans above the frank?" Ted's humiliation is compounded when Charlie calls in Mary's mom, Sheila. Like any well-intentioned mom would do, Sheila applies a little Bactine to the wound. Ted's excruciating pain and horrifying embarrassment, as well as the hilarity of the situation, escalates as the bathroom becomes more crowded with the arrival of the police and fire department, all expressing their utter disbelief at Ted's predicament.

Proof that truth is sometimes stranger than fiction, the bathroom scene was based on a real-life event that happened at a party when the Farrellys were growing up in Rhode Island. One of the partygoers got himself into a similarly painful pinch and the Farrellys' parents had to come to his rescue.

It is revealed that Ted is reliving these painfully embarrassing high school moments as he recounts them in a session with his psychiatrist. It's obvious that Ted is still carrying a torch for his old high school flame, Mary.

For solace, Ted turns to his close friend Woogie, played by comic actor Chris Elliot. Unaware that Woogie is also infatuated with Mary, Ted takes his advice and hires a private investigator to track her down. The sleazy private eye Pat Healy, played by Matt Dillon, finds Mary living in Florida and promptly falls in love with her himself. He then lies to Ted, describing Mary as an obese, handicapped single mom, when in fact she's beautiful, fit, and successful. Healy stalks Mary and assumes the false identity of an architect in order to date her. There's just something about Mary that attracts obsessive losers. The role of the shady P.I. required a checked ego for Dillon, who sported a cheesy, pencil-thin mustache and huge false teeth to personify the smarmy imposter.

Meanwhile, Ted discovers that

Healy deceived him, and he drives to Florida to win Mary's love. Disenchanted with Healy, Mary agrees to go out on a date with Ted.

The Farrellys tackle a risqué subject indeed when Woogie counsels Ted that if he doesn't "clean his pipes" before going on the date with Mary, it's like he would be going out "with a loaded gun." So Ted takes Woogie's brotherly advice and addresses the problem in the bathroom before his date with Mary. A potentially vulgar moment was again rendered hysterically funny by pacing and scoring the action to the growing crescendo from the opera *Carmen*. Stiller's contorted face and the roll of his eyes upon climax heightened the silliness of the scene.

It's funnier still when, surprisingly, Ted finds nothing to clean up, only to be mortified when he opens the door to greet Mary and discovers there's something dangling from his ear. "Is that . . . is that hair gel?" Mary asks, as she grabs it and applies it to her own hair. In the next scene at dinner, Mary, sitting

with a stiffened "swoop" of hair standing straight up in the air above her forehead, became an iconic movie image of the '90s.

Cameron Diaz was incredulous about the scene, telling the Farrellys that any woman would know the difference between hair gel and the actual substance in question. So the brothers tested the scene before a focus group and found that it was not only perceived as believable, but—more important—good for big laughs. It has become the emblematic moment of the movie and one to be counted among the funniest in modern film history.

The sometimes-offensive humor and unabashed vulgarity of the movie received its share of criticism, with some reviewers even dubbing *There's Something About Mary* a "gross-out film." But by Hollywood standards, the only gross that really matters relates to box office. The $13.7 million the movie earned in its opening weekend, and the more than $360 million it earned worldwide during its theatrical run, proved that there really was something about Mary beyond the crude and outlandish content.

GROSS-OUT MOMENTS

Many directors have discovered that the grosser their film, the more their film grosses. Here are examples of films that took lowbrow to high art.

Blazing Saddles (1974) Intentional or not, every gratuitous gassy moment in movies today is an homage to Mel Brooks's *Blazing Saddles*. In a film full of tasteless, politically incorrect humor, the backfire around the campfire is a standout. As a harmonica whines a lonely prairie tune, cowpokes eat their bean dinners around the campfire. Suddenly, one by one, they raise themselves up just enough to allow a flatulent flutter to resonate across the open range. This is the scene that put the "blazing" in *Blazing Saddles*.

Caddyshack (1980) To the ominous strains of the shark's theme from *Jaws*, a Baby Ruth bar is spotted floating in the swimming pool at the hoity-toity Bushwood Country Club. When everyone around the pool assumes it's fecal matter, they flee the pool in a panic. Their horror is compounded when goofball groundskeeper Carl Spackler, played by Bill Murray, drains the pool, examines the candy bar, and eats it.

Airplane! (1980) This spoof of 1970s disaster movies is chock-full of raunch and double entendre–laced dialogue. When the passengers and crew are stricken by food poisoning, airhead flight attendant Elaine (Julie Hagerty) discovers that the automatic pilot—an inflatable man in a pilot suit—is deflating. She doesn't know what to do, so the implacable air-traffic controller McCrosky (Lloyd Bridges) guides her from the ground. "On the belt line of the automatic pilot there's a tube. Now that is the manual inflation nozzle. Take it out and blow on it." Elaine dutifully follows directions and the automatic pilot reinflates, sporting a satisfied smile on his face.

American Pie (1999) In the hilarious tradition of *Porky's*, *Fast Times At Ridgemont High*, and *Dazed and Confused*, a quartet of pals in *American Pie* are on a single-minded mission to slip under the sheets and into manhood by prom night—or bust. One of the many line-treading moments in the film occurs when Jim arrives home to find a fresh baked apple pie on the kitchen counter with a note from his mother saying she won't be home till late. After inserting his fingers through the crust and into the pie's warm, moist center, Jim's libido and perverse curiosity surge into overdrive. Jim's father (Eugene Levy) unwittingly arrives home to find his son having his way with the tart. As the violated pastry lies in front of them, Jim's father offers, "Well, we'll just tell your mother that we ate it all." The scene inspired the movies slogan, "You never forget your first slice."

CAST AWAY

2000

When Charlie Chaplin made his last silent film *Modern Times* in 1936, he was already swimming against the tide. The first "talkies" had appeared in 1929, and by the time Chaplin's lovable tramp stumbled through his final pratfall, the Silent Era had breathed its last. So it was with understandable jitters that, nearly seventy-five years later, 20th Century Fox gave the green light to *Cast Away,* a costly project that featured its star acting nearly wordlessly for most of the movie.

What they got was Tom Hanks's bravura portrayal of Chuck Noland, a Federal Express troubleshooter who survives a horrendous plane crash in the Pacific Ocean and a four-year struggle for survival on a deserted island with only a volleyball he's named Wilson for companionship. When he's ultimately rescued, Noland is forced to come to terms with a life that has passed him by. It was a tour de force depiction that wowed most critics and prompted a major New York daily to proclaim it "one of the towering screen perform-ances of all time."

Not only did director Robert Zemeckis's modern-day Robinson Crusoe tale shock the studio brass by raking in enough to make it the second-highest-grossing film of 2000 and one of the top twenty-five earners of all time, it also involved an unprecedented yearlong break in production during which Hanks underwent a grueling physical transformation. After three months of filming, the forty-three-year-old actor gave up haircuts, grew a chest-length mane, and dropped fifty pounds before resuming the role.

What made the film extraordinary, apart from the

compelling acting and first-rate production work of Zemeckis and his crew, was that Hanks spent two-thirds of the picture's 140-minute running time on screen alone—cracking coconuts, hunting fish, chopping trees, and building fires—an extremely difficult proposition for any actor. The star would later say it was an excruciating experience, one that left him bruised and battered, and with a staph infection in his leg that nearly led to his death from blood poisoning. "They don't make movies like this very often, and now we know why," Hanks quipped during the filming. "It's very hard!"

With the help of screenwriter William Broyles Jr., who had scripted the successful 1995 Hanks film *Apollo 13,* the actor had begun work on his pet project years earlier, after seeing a TV news report on an American soldier shipwrecked during World War II. Hanks concluded that a similar tale of loneliness and isolation would give him a unique opportunity to stretch his abilities as an actor. The two produced a preliminary draft—the script would ultimately go through 125 rewrites–and brought it to Zemeckis, with whom Hanks had worked on the 1994 Oscar-winning *Forrest Gump.*

The director was intrigued but was unsure about how to account for the passage of time in the story. Four years of gobbling minnows and drinking coconut milk exacts a physical toll on a man, and both Hanks and Zemeckis knew the success of the project would rest on a true depiction of the ravages of such an attenuating existence. They realized that the only solution was to shoot the film in two parts. The first would feature a rather pudgy Hanks going about his FedEx job, courting his girlfriend, Kelly, played by Helen Hunt, surviving a harrowing plane crash, and learning to live on the

island. The second would be shot a year later, giving Hanks time to transform himself, and would focus on his escape from the island on a homemade raft, his rescue, and his bittersweet homecoming.

When Zemeckis presented his agenda to executives at 20th Century Fox, it was met with raised eyebrows. They were less than thrilled with the idea of a sixteen-month production schedule during which the crew would spend nearly fifty weeks twiddling their thumbs while Hanks went through his transformation—the studio would be forced to shell out a small fortune just to keep everyone on retainer. So Zemeckis took a novel approach: He would film the initial portion of *Cast Away* in early 1999, then, while Hanks went on hiatus, the director and the *Cast Away* crew would shoot another picture for Fox, resuming work on *Cast Away*

in early 2000. The studio consented, granting a $90 million budget to each film, and between August and December of 1999, Zemeckis churned out *What Lies Beneath,* a Hitchcockian thriller starring Harrison Ford and Michelle Pfeiffer. In February, they returned to work with Hanks.

While *Cast Away*'s filming locations Ping-Ponged from Moscow and Memphis to Los Angeles and Texas, the majority of shooting—and certainly the most grueling part—took place on and around the far-flung island of Monuriki in Fiji. Hanks and the 120-member crew were forced to bear a litany of elemental abuses—thunderstorms, shifting tides, bugs, scorching heat—with only a few hastily constructed plywood huts for protection. The daily boat trip to and from their hotel on another island was nearly three hours long.

The rugged conditions brought out the primordial best in Hanks. Noland must use the limited resources at his disposal to re-create civilization. In one of the film's most memorable sequences, we witness a beleaguered Noland rubbing two sticks together in a futile attempt to create fire. Day turns to night and night to day, and finally, palms blistered and bones weary, he gives up. It is clear that Noland's notion of survivalism comes straight from Hollywood, where sparking a roaring blaze in the wild is as easy as pitching a tent.

At this point, fate intervenes. After accidentally cracking one of the switches—a necessity for creating the flame—Noland succeeds. Dancing maniacally and waving flaming palm fronds around his new bonfire, he screams to his mute surroundings, "Look what I have created! I have made fire! I have made fire!" The scene represented Noland's first major success on the island, and Hanks played it with impressively demented style as the modern man who has temporarily reverted to the level of his less-erect ancestors.

The scene is also the first in which Noland speaks to "Wilson," a volleyball that washed up in a FedEx package after the plane crash. Noland throws the ball in a rage of frustration while trying to spark his fire, leaving his own bloody palm print on its surface. Once calm, he anthropomorphized the ball by scratching a face into the palm print. Wilson becomes Noland's faithful companion on the island.

The idea for Wilson came from screenwriter Broyles, who felt Hanks needed a sounding board so that the island scenes would not be completely devoid of dialogue; Broyles even toyed with the concept of bringing the ball to life in Noland's imagination and having it speak. In the end, the volleyball remained mute, although according to Hanks, Wilson actually had dozens of lines of dialogue that were never heard but to which he responded.

In lesser hands, the relationship would probably

carry a strong whiff of slapstick comedy, but Hanks managed to bring it off with disarming pathos, particularly in the heartrending scene in which he must abandon his "friend" on the high seas just before his rescue.

For his convincing and compelling depiction of Chuck Noland's four-year island odyssey, Hanks, as expected, collected acting nominations from almost every major body, and walked off with the Golden Globe. Although the Academy passed on *Cast Away* for Best Picture, it was nominated for Best Actor and Sound, losing in both categories.

Cast Away's minimal dialogue inspired director Robert Zemeckis to call it "a silent movie with sound"—proof that old-fashioned storytelling could still cast a spell.

TOM HANKS MOMENTS

The Jimmy Stewart of his generation, Oscar winner Tom Hanks is a gifted actor who can play a wide range of characters. Here are some of his more memorable roles.

Big (1988) "Be careful what you wish for . . ." is the theme of this Hanks comedy that earned him his first Best Actor Oscar nomination. As thirteen-year-old Josh Baskin watches an older guy pick up the girl of his dreams, he puts a quarter in a carnival machine and makes a wish: "I wish I was big." Poof! The next morning his wish comes true, and while Josh is finding his way as a kid trapped in a grown-up's body, he winds up in a toy store performing a crowd-pleasing version of "Heart and Soul" on a floor-sized piano keyboard alongside MacMillan (Robert Loggia), a toy company president and his future boss. Hanks hit all the right notes, and *Big* was a big success.

Philadelphia (1993) Andrew Beckett (Hanks), a promising hotshot attorney at a prestigious Philadelphia law firm, is unceremoniously fired after his conservative bosses discover he's not only homosexual, but he also has AIDS. To fight what he believes is a wrongful termination, he hires attorney Joe Miller (Denzel Washington). While Miller struggles to overcome his own feelings of homophobia, he becomes an unlikely ally in Andrew's battle for his dignity and the fight for his life. This remarkable film explores life's complexities associated with the insidious disease and the courage to come to terms with its decisive prognosis, earning Hanks his first Best Actor Oscar.

Forrest Gump (1994) Hanks's triumphant performance as the big-hearted dullard Forrest Gump earned him his second consecutive Best Actor Oscar. By happenstance, Gump, whose motto is "Life is like a box of chocolates: You never know what you're going to get," finds himself at the center of most of the seminal moments of the last half of the twentieth century. The impressive special effects employed to place Gump in newsreel footage with Presidents John F. Kennedy and Richard Nixon provides for some of the film's funnier moments.

Apollo 13 (1995) With the calm declaration "Houston, we have a problem," astronaut James Lovell marked the beginning of one of the most traumatic stories in the history of manned space flight, and the near-disastrous moon mission of *Apollo 13* became the subject of this unforgettable film. As *Apollo 13* rocketed toward the moon, an oxygen tank exploded, crippling the ship and leaving the crew of James Lovell, Fred Haise, and Jack Swigert stranded in space 200,000 miles from Earth. Hanks's portrayal of astronaut Lovell palpably captured the trio's seesawing emotions as the men desperately clung to hope.

Saving Private Ryan (1998) This World War II epic directed by Steven Spielberg tells the traumatic story of a unit of U.S. soldiers, led by Captain John Miller (Tom Hanks), sent behind enemy lines to find Private James Ryan (Matt Damon). Ryan's three brothers have been killed in action, and Miller's mission is to track down Ryan before he meets the same fate. In the film's first twenty minutes director Spielberg re-creates the Normandy invasion with harrowing realism. On a grand cinematic scale, *Saving Private Ryan* demonstrated both the horror and the heroism that is war.

THE LORD OF THE RINGS

2001/2002

When the first book in the Lord of the Rings trilogy was originally published in 1954, neither author J. R. R. Tolkien nor his readers could have imagined that the carefully crafted mythology would grow into one of the most widely read and beloved works of modern fiction.

That enduring devotion from generations of readers who journeyed to the fantasy world of "Middle Earth," where the fate of all that is good rests on the small shoulders of a three-foot-tall, pointed-eared, furry-footed creature called a hobbit, made the motion picture release of *The Fellowship of the Ring* one of the most highly anticipated films of all time.

The Fellowship of the Ring could count itself as one of the most successful movies in motion picture history, grossing more than $800 million worldwide.

But even before the film's debut, *The Lord of the Rings* marked a remarkable first in the history of film-making. It had been shot in an aura of secrecy. Industry trade papers and Internet sites were abuzz with excitement. And in a day and age where very little lives up to its hype, director Peter Jackson knew that this long-awaited movie version of the trilogy ran the huge risk of disappointing millions of Tolkien fans around the world. Much to the contrary, the film was greeted with virtually unanimous praise.

From its very inception, the film was an arduous trek for Jackson, who had earned an Oscar nomination for screenwriting on his 1994 film *Heavenly Creatures* and achieved cult status with the grisly horror thriller

Braindead. The prime mover behind bringing Middle Earth to the screen, Jackson wanted to make the film ever since reading the books at the age of eighteen. But most of Hollywood executives did not share Jackson's passion and balked at the idea of producing more than one movie out of the three books. Jackson believed it an injustice not to produce the film in separate installments and took the project to New Line Cinema, where executive producer Mark Ordesky encouraged him to make the film as a trilogy.

And so Jackson and his team embarked on a daunting and formidable task of unprecedented enormity: to shoot three films back to back, with cast and crew living together for sixteen months on location. Never had such an ambitious endeavor been attempted, and Jackson himself said he felt as if they were "in constant danger of the train derailing." After all, he knew that Ralph Bakshi's 1978 effort at turning Tolkien's words into an animated movie was generally considered a flop, never making it past the first installment.

By contrast, Jackson envisioned Middle Earth as a real, three-dimensional world inhabited by living flesh-and-blood creatures. He chose his homeland of New Zealand for the setting. The dramatic snow-capped landscapes and the pastoral wilderness harkened back to an era unspoiled by industry and development, much like the rural England that still existed at the time of Tolkien's writings.

The cast was meticulously assembled. Venerable British actor Ian McKellen would play the noble wizard Gandalf the Grey, charged with protecting the people of Middle Earth from evil. Gandalf is also the protector of a hobbit named Frodo Baggins, embodied by Elijah Wood, who must take the accursed ring of power back to the fires of Mount Doom, where it was forged. Only there can it be destroyed and thus the world be saved. Gandalf and Frodo are joined by the scruffy Aragorn, the self-exiled heir to the throne of the race of men, played by Viggo Mortensen. Along with expert archer Legolas the Elf (Orlando Bloom), axe-wielding Gimli the Dwarf

(John Rhys-Davies), three more hobbits, and another warrior, they become the Fellowship of the Ring.

The road to Mount Doom is fraught with peril. A legion of snarling bloodthirsty Orcs, goblins, and the occasional cave troll try to destroy the fellowship, under orders from a dark lord who desires the ring of power to rule the world.

The cast and crew knew that they had signed on for a once-in-a-lifetime opportunity on a scale that none had ever experienced in making a motion picture. Each admitted they became completely immersed in their role, and none more so than Mortensen, who was not the first choice to play the stoic yet gallant Aragorn. Mortensen became so thoroughly dedicated to the character that he carried his medieval-looking sword wherever he went in New Zealand, unwittingly scaring some of the local townspeople. Looking like a crazed sword-wielding monk, still half-clad as Aragorn, he was confronted by police one day as he walked back to his car from rehearsal.

Ian McKellen summed up the collective sentiment among cast and crew, describing his own feelings when he first saw the rows of hobbit homes built into the hillside. "The Tolkien trilogy is a fairy tale," McKellen told an interviewer. "It didn't happen, except in our hearts. But there was Hobbiton, with smoke pouring out of the holes . . . and I believed."

In creating that mystical setting, Tolkien wrote descriptions in such tremendous detail—about the environment, the cultures, and even the languages—that his epic story of good versus evil seemed more like ancient history than a fairy tale. Peter Jackson's edict to the set builders was to embrace that very notion that the people and places described in Tolkien's tales had really once existed. That unswerving dedication became a big asset in moving the production forward, as the crew could rely on Tolkien's own words to create sets, props, and costumes while the screenwriting was still in process.

Attention to the script was an integral part of the production, and there were countless rewrites. Jackson and cowriters Fran Walsh and Phillipe Boyens regretted that some aspects from the books had to be cut, but they went to agonizing lengths to preserve the crucial elements needed to advance the story. It wasn't unusual for members of the cast to wake up after an arduous day of rehearsals only to find several pages of revisions had been slid under their doors during the night.

Nothing was left to chance. In addition to the meticulous attention to the script, frame-by-frame hand-illustrated storyboards were made of virtually every shot. Then a 3-D computer technique called pre-visualization was employed. Jackson and company actually visited the Lucasfilm ranch in Northern California, the birthplace of many modern special effects, to see its state-of-the-art previsualization technology. They then adapted that technology—in renderings that looked like 3-D video games—to map out the big sweeping scenes that would become emblematic of the production, all this before even shooting a foot of film.

It's no small irony that the production would rely heavily on state-of-the-art computer-generated effects in order to make Tolkien's ancient fantasy world come to life. More than five hundred visual effects were shot for the first film alone, and many of the most memorable scenes from the film were the most complicated.

First, the critical issue of scale had to be addressed and resolved. That is, men and elves are about six feet tall and Hobbits are only three feet in height, but in reality Elijah Wood and Ian McKellen are not that disparate in height. The problem was solved both by tried-and-tested illusions of camera angle and perspective and with digital superimposition of the actors' faces over small stunt doubles.

Various state-of-the-art effects were employed in the unforgettable and perhaps most dramatic confrontation of the first film. The Fellowship is fleeing down the seemingly endless stairs deep within the ancient mines of Moria in order to cross the Bridge of Khazad-dum. The set, which looks like a cross between the Tomb Raider video game and an intricate geometric puzzle that surrealist M. C. Escher would have drawn, was actually an elaborate miniature model that was scanned and then reproduced with digital computer graphics. The movements of the actors were recorded in the studio through motion-capture cameras and then "digital doubles" of the characters were inserted into the computer-generated shot. The result is a thoroughly believable, action-packed race through the depths of the middle earth in order to escape a fiery demon.

One of the film's most ferocious creatures is called a Balrog. It moves with the bravado of Charles Atlas in the form of a gigantic fire-breathing demon. Fire oozes

from the cracks in the scales of his skin. As our heroes run across the narrow stone Bridge of Khazad-dum, Gandalf the wizard stays behind to confront the demon.

Jackson and his crew of movie magicians were able to pull off this enormous effect by choosing not to digitally synthesize the eruptions of flame pouring from the monster, but rather to film real patterns and particles of fire. Then the computer-generated Balrog was inserted into the shot as the force behind those flames. It took a month of research and development and six weeks of nonstop production to execute this battle between wizard and beast.

As actor Ian McKellen raises both staff and sword to ward off the blows from the Balrog's whip of fire, he shouts, "You shall not pass!" in a flawless representation of the scene as written by Tolkien. The old wizard displays great power as the bridge crumbles beneath the weight of the approaching beast. As the Balrog falls into the abyss, it catches the wizard off guard and he too tumbles into the darkness below.

The second installment of the trilogy, *The Two Towers,* opens with Gandalf and the Balrog hurtling downward into the deepening void. The gray wizard catches his sword in mid-air to smite the demon as they soar deeper and deeper into the depths of the mountain.

It is also in the second film that we are formally introduced to Gollum, the slithering cutthroat creature who also desires the ring of power. He creeps up on the

hobbits Frodo and Samwise and attacks them in their sleep. The ensuing fight between the hobbits and Gollum is so realistic it is dumbfounding to learn that this creature is also computer-generated. But not entirely.

The fiendish Gollum was originally conceived as a computer-generated character, with actor Andy Serkis simply providing the voice. But Serkis's audition for the part was so compelling that Jackson decided to shoot Serkis acting in every scene while wearing a skintight Lycra suit, eventually to be replaced by the computer image. The result is a performance that makes the inanimate Gollum remarkably real. In fact, Serkis's vocal work and the computer character are so convincing that the self-loathing, murderous creature becomes one of the most sympathetic and tragic of all the characters in the saga.

When the first of the three films, *The Fellowship of the Ring,* was finally ready for theatrical release in December 2001 and premiered in London and Los Angeles, thousands of fans lined the streets. But when the film premiered in Wellington, New Zealand, the entire city came out in droves to honor Peter Jackson, the cast, and the crew. The country of New Zealand could take great pride knowing it had played a significant role in a landmark motion picture achievement. In fact, the city even changed its name for the day. Wellington was now officially *Middle Earth.*

CGI CHARACTERS

The one-hundred-plus years of motion picture history are marked by innovations that have made the moviegoing experience ever more thrilling. First *motion* pictures themselves, then sound, then color, and now computer-generated imagery, or CGI. The character of Gollum in *The Lord of the Rings: The Two Towers* has been lauded as the best example to date of the union of technology and art in moviemaking. As lifelike as Gollum appears, however, it still took the human touch of actor Andy Serkis to give Gollum his soul. Here are more examples where state-of-the-art CGI artistry and good old-fashioned acting resulted in unforgettable characters.

Toy Story (1995) The first totally computer-generated feature film was a coproduction of Disney and CGI pioneers Pixar Studios. It's the story of toys that come to life in a young boy's bedroom when humans aren't around. Woody, a pull-string cowboy doll, is Andy's favorite and the leader of all the other toys in Andy's room. That is, until Buzz Lightyear arrives on Andy's birthday. Buzz is a Space Ranger action figure not about to be bossed around by a beat-up cowpoke, turning Woody's world upside down. Despite the remarkable three-dimensional CGI animation, it's the personalities in the voices of Tom Hanks (Woody) and Tim Allen (Buzz) that make these characters so endearing. The movie captured the hearts and imagination of parents and children alike, and animation would never be the same. To infinity—and beyond!

Shrek (2001) This is the story of affable ogre Shrek, whose serene swamp home, surrounded by KEEP OUT and BEWARE THE OGRE! signs, suddenly becomes a refuge for fairy tale characters banished into exile by the evil Lord Farquaad. Only when Shrek agrees to bring Princess Fiona to Lord Farquaad will he help Shrek with his fairy tale–character infestation. *Shrek* was the box office hit of 2001. It took more than 275 artists, software developers, and computer animators three years to complete the film. Sophisticated computer tools called shapers were used to create realistic facial expressions and make the clothing, hair, and fur of the characters appear to move naturally over their bone structure. But technical breakthroughs don't make the story of an ogre engaging; an edgy script and the talented voices of Mike Myers as Shrek, John Lithgow as Lord Farquaad, Cameron Diaz as the fair Princess Fiona, and Eddie Murphy as Shrek's faithful sidekick Donkey make this wicked, funny story a classic.

Monsters, Inc. (2001) The netherworld of Monstropolis is fueled by the collected screams of human children. Sulley, a giant blue-furred monster employed by Monster's, Inc., the largest scream refinery in the monster world, is the best in the scare business. Sulley and his assistant, one-eyed Mike Wazowski, have their hands full when a two-year-old girl called Boo accidentally sneaks into the monsters' world, where humans are considered toxic. In their fourth film together, Disney and Pixar Studios pushed the envelop of CGI technology. Among the many breakthroughs is the depiction of nearly three million single strands of hair on Sulley's feathery coat. The film required two and a half million renderings (a measure of computing power), compared to *Toy Story 2*, which required less than half as many. Actor John Goodman gave Sulley his heart and soul, saying that Sulley reminded him of one of those "old NFL guys in the tenth year of his career, totally dedicated and a total pro." Billy Crystal was the voice of Mike and imagined his character to be "Burgess Meredith to John Goodman's Rocky."

Finding Nemo (2003) When a little clown fish named Nemo is captured near his home on the Great Barrier Reef, his dad, Marlin, sets out on a perilous journey to find him. Along the way, Marlin is befriended by Dory, a well-intentioned yet forgetful blue tang. This all-CGI feature was Disney and Pixar's fifth and most challenging collaboration. The realistic underwater environment required development of still newer technologies to simulate the complexities of the ocean floor; the color, reflections, and refractions of the light streaming down from the water's surface; the debris in the water; the constant shift in the underwater current; and the murkiness in the distant background. For inspiration, animators had a twenty-five-gallon aquarium installed in their office, allowing them to study clown fish, blue tangs, and other species. The comedic sensibilities of actors Albert Brooks (Marlin), Ellen DeGeneres (Dory), and newcomer Alexander Gould (Nemo) also provided inspiration. The movie became the highest-grossing computer-animated film and set a new high-water mark in CGI animation.

Photo Credits

Other Credits

Authored, produced, and directed by Joe Garner.

Editorial/text assistance provided by Stephan Michaels, Stuart Miller, Todd Schindler, and Bill Stroum.

Narration written by Mark Rowland.

Footage, music, and talent clearances managed by The Clearance House.

Original musical score composed and orchestrated by Richard Kosinski.

Studio production facilities provided by the Production Group Studio, Hollywood, California.

Director of photography and associate director: Kris Wilson

Production coordinator and assistant to Joe Garner: Abigail Ray

DVD chapters edited by Chris Monte, Magic Hair, Inc.

Assistant editor: Jason Cherella

Assistant editor/motion control: Jason Chaney

Audio production engineer: Mike Forslund

Main title, animation, and menu design: Castle Digital Design

Creative director: James Castle

Senior animator: Robert Dixon

DVD authoring provided by Los Angeles Duplication and Broadcast, Burbank, California.

Motion picture clips provided by and copyright of:

The Godfather Part II courtesy of Paramount Pictures

Raiders of the Lost Ark courtesy of Paramount Pictures and Lucasfilm, Ltd

The Exorcist and *Dirty Harry* courtesy of Warner Bros.

The Wizard of Oz and *Casablanca* courtesy of Turner Entertainment Co.

Five Easy Pieces and *On the Waterfront* courtesy of Columbia Pictures

Silence of the Lambs © 1991 Orion Pictures Corporation

Rocky © 1976 Metro-Goldwyn-Mayer Studios Inc.

Some Like It Hot © 1959 Metro-Goldwyn-Mayer Studios Inc.

Thelma & Louise © 1991 Metro-Goldwyn-Mayer Studios Inc. courtesy of MGM CLIP+STILL

Alien, Cast Away, There's Something About Mary, and *Wall Street* courtesy of 20th Century Fox Film Corporation

Psycho, E.T.: The Extra-Terrestrial, Jaws, National Lampoon's Animal House, and *Field of Dreams* courtesy of Universal Studios Licensing LLP

When Harry Met Sally courtesy Castle Rock Entertainment

The Graduate courtesy of StudioCanal Image

Pulp Fiction courtesy of Miramax Film

The Lord of the Rings: The Fellowship of the Ring courtesy of New Line Productions Inc. © 2001 New Line Productions Inc.
TM The Saul Zaentz Company d/b/a Tolkien Enterprises under license to New Line Productions, Inc. All rights reserved.

The Lord of the Rings: The Two Towers courtesy of New Line Productions Inc. © 2002 New Line Productions Inc.
TM The Saul Zaentz Company d/b/a Tolkien Enterprises under license to New Line Productions Inc. All rights reserved.

Performance of Humphrey Bogart is licensed through TM/©2003 Bogart, Inc. by www.CMGWorldwide.com.

Performance of Ingrid Bergman is licensed through TM/©2003 Family of Ingrid Bergman by www.CMGWorldwide.com.

Performance of Marilyn Monroe is licensed through TM/©2003 Marilyn Monroe LLC by www.CMGWorldwide.com, www.MarilynMonroe.com.

A very special thank-you to all of the actors and actresses who have graciously permitted the inclusion of their performances.